BACKTALK

FOUR STEPS TO ENDING
RUDE BEHAVIOR
IN YOUR KIDS

**Audrey Ricker, Ph.D.,
and Carolyn Crowder, Ph.D.**

A FIRESIDE BOOK
PUBLISHED BY SIMON & SCHUSTER

F

FIRESIDE
Rockefeller Center
1230 Avenue of the Americas
New York, NY 10020

FIRESIDE and colophon are registered trademarks
of Simon & Schuster Inc.

Designed by Jennifer Ann Daddio

Manufactured in the United States of America

5   7   9   10   8   6

Library of Congress Cataloging-in-Publication Data
Ricker, Audrey.
Backtalk : four steps to ending rude behavior in your kids / Audrey Ricker and
Carolyn Crowder.
p.   cm.
"A Fireside book."
Includes index.
1. Child rearing. 2. Parent and child. 3. Discipline of children. 4. Children —
Conduct of life. 5. Respect. Crowder, Carolyn Zoe. II. Title.
HQ769.R52   1998
649'.64 — dc21   97-36549
CIP

ISBN 0-684-84124-X

To Henrietta Terrazas-Dyer, a model mother, and to Ana, Alex, and Carlos Terrazas, her model children

A.R.

To Dr. Oscar Christensen, who has taught so many about respectful relationships with children

C.C.

CONTENTS

AUTHOR'S NOTE

When I began studying psychology, the theory of behavior that made the most sense to me was one developed by Alfred Adler. Although he wrote at the turn of the century, Adler's philosophy is surprisingly pertinent to modern-day problems. Adlerian psychology provides the basis for this book. If you don't understand this theory as you begin to read, come back to it when you finish. The following information will be more understandable to you at that time.

Adler—and later, his disciple, Rudolf Dreikurs—believed the most important point to make to parents was that their reaction to a child's misbehavior would either (1) encourage the behavior, resulting in its recurrence, or (2) discourage the behavior. In other words, a parent's response makes all the difference.

Adler felt that children misbehave in order to find significance in the family. A child who cannot find a sense of belonging through positive behavior will choose negative actions. By belonging in a positive sense, I do not mean the child is made the center of attention. Belonging positively includes cooperating with, contributing to, and having empathy for others. When children backtalk and get a reaction from their parents such as "You can't talk to me that way" or

"You better watch it or I'll . . .", they learn that backtalk brings them attention, power, and often a way of hurting their parents.

This ability to get attention, albeit negative, to dominate, or to get back at parental figures makes the child feel significant. But this is a negative significance and we want our children to feel positive significance. We make a big difference by the way we respond to their misbehavior.

This book provides a way for you to respond to backtalk that will allow children to find ways to belong positively, not just in the family but everywhere else as well.

Our four-step system is an example of the Adlerian idea of logical consequences put into practice. A logical consequence is just that—a consequence that is a result of the misbehavior. It is not punishment because it is not arbitrary, and it never involves screaming, threatening, spanking, sarcasm, or lecturing. When parents consistently follow through with logical consequences, children learn that parents mean what they say and will follow through.

As an Adlerian, I feel I ought to stress the need to provide ways for our children to find positive significance, especially through making a real contribution to the family as a whole. Simple actions—helping to prepare a meal or plan a vacation and pitching in when a parent or sibling is sick—build feelings of significance and empathy. So, as you find yourself responding constructively to backtalk, think of ways to involve your children in contributing to others.

C.C.

INTRODUCTION

If you picked up this book, chances are you are having trouble with backtalk from your children. You've probably been told that you shouldn't pay attention to it, that it's just the way children express themselves these days.

But our position is that you should do something about it. Your children need you to do something about it. With this book as your guide, you will learn a pattern of responding that will enable you to deal with backtalk immediately, every time it happens. When children are allowed to get away with backtalk, they don't learn to have respect for others.

Dr. Ricker wanted to write this book because she saw that her students' backtalk was completely out of hand, whether they were in elementary school or college. As a mother she had to deal with backtalk. She saw that firm consequences not only eliminated the backtalk problem but also helped the child.

Dr. Crowder, a psychologist and parent trainer, has long wanted to provide a theoretical and behavioral framework for handling this problem. In her parenting classes she has observed that nearly all parents are confused about, and feel helpless in, handling their children's backtalk.

This book is aimed at preventing backtalk. Parents, teachers, and other adults who deal with children will find that the book provides a clear, simple method of responding to the problem. This response consists of a Four-Step Program that anyone can use, with consistent practice.

Here is a scenario that shows how backtalk can strike for the first time when it is least expected.

Case History #1: The Jones family was gathered in the living room watching television and reading while Mary Jones grilled hamburgers for dinner. Mary and John Jones are both physicians, the eleven-year-old twin boys are soccer players, and sixteen-year-old Joe is an honor student and track star. The rapport that Mary and John enjoy with their children is the envy of all their friends.

On this particular night Mrs. Jones came in to ask how everyone wanted his hamburger cooked, medium or well done?

"Medium," said one twin.

"Same," said the other.

"Medium well," said John.

"Joe?" asked Mary. "What about you?"

Silence. Joe did not even turn and look at her.

"Joe? How about your burger?" Mary prompted cheerfully.

"I'm *watching* this *show*," Joe said, his tone full of annoyance. "Can't you see that? God!" He then turned his attention back to the television, ignoring his mother completely.

Joe's response to his mother included the following characteristics: sudden rudeness, nasty tone, inflected syllables, hostility, and bullying control of the conversation. In other words, Joe started the backtalk attack without provocation, he controlled the nature of the attack, and he ended it when he decided to. Mary never knew what hit her!

At this point, parents like Mary and John typically see only two possible responses — either to ignore the attack or to escalate the negative exchange, neither of which will help to solve the problem. In doing nothing constructive, the parents are left wondering where they went wrong and the twins are being influenced by their older brother's rude behavior.

However, there is another way to handle the situation. The parents in this example could use the steps we've outlined in this book to stop this backtalk and future attacks. It pays to be prepared to deal with backtalk before it happens. If you've already experienced it in your household, it's not too late to manage it successfully. The fact is, rude behavior *needs* parental intervention and being allowed to get away with backtalk is bad for your child.

Backtalk can ruin a person's chances for a productive, happy life, because a child who gets away with it at home will undoubtedly try backtalking outside the home, losing respect of friends, friends' parents, teachers, and, later, employers. At home he can be ostracized by parents who don't know how else to deal with him. He could even be sent away by adults who have no idea of how to deal with the behavior. At school, he could become known as a difficult child whom adults and children avoid. Later, on the job, his backtalk could keep him from getting and keeping promotions.

Parents are not the only household members affected by

backtalk; younger or less dominant siblings become intimi-dated. They soon learn how to respond in kind, and backtalk becomes the model of communication in the home. If back-talk is allowed to continue unchecked, the atmosphere in the home will become hostile, unsettling, and discouraging for the whole family. And a few backtalkers in the classroom can ruin a teacher's ability to teach.

Parents can learn to distinguish between backtalk and respectful disagreement. *Autocratic* families may be eager to see all disagreement from children as backtalk. *Permissive* families accept the verbal abuse as legitimate communication. *Assertive communication* is respectful while backtalk is never respectful. Backtalk includes not only disrespectful words, but a disrespectful tone and disrespectful body language as well. Any or all of these manifestations of backtalk should be addressed by parents.

WHAT THIS BOOK WILL DO

Backtalk will help parents learn how to have a backtalk-free home. It's normal to feel hurt, angry, and disappointed by chil-dren's backtalk. A constructive approach to dealing with these feelings is provided here. Unlike other child-rearing books, which encourage you to view backtalk as healthy communi-cation, this book will treat backtalk for what it is—disre-spectful behavior—and teach parents how to handle backtalk when it happens. Here is a chapter-by-chapter overview:

In Part One, "What, Why, When, and How," we explain, among other things, what backtalk is, why it has become an epidemic, when it became legitimized by child-rearing experts, and how it affects families, schools, and the backtalkers themselves. Part I also explains what you can do about backtalk, why you must do something, when you should do it, and how.

In Chapter 1, "Frank Talk About Backtalk," we discuss the pleasures of the backtalk-free home, the nature of backtalk, and reasons for dealing with it in a timely fashion. This chapter shows you how to identify this problem and explains briefly which conditions in our culture, especially the growth of mainstream media, have helped backtalk reach epidemic proportions in the past few years. Chapter 2 explains the Four-Step Program for dealing with backtalk, discussing the steps in detail and providing a variety of case histories.

In Part Two, "Practice," we provide instructions for implementing the steps for dealing with backtalk. In this section we also discuss and validate attitude problems adults often have in implementing the Four-Step Program. We cover issues you may encounter as you apply the four steps to children of different ages, including college age and adult children. You'll learn how to deal with teachers, caregivers, psychologists, and adult relatives who may disapprove of your stand on backtalk, and we'll also examine the unique backtalk problems faced by single parents and working couples. We'll discuss how to deal with your child's backtalking friends, and what to do about other external sources of backtalk including movies and television. Part Two also includes a chapter on creating and maintaining a backtalk workbook in which you can track the effectiveness of the Four-Step Program and keep a list of solutions that work for you. Finally, we'll recommend support groups to join and types to avoid, and we'll tell you how to start one of your own.

SUGGESTIONS FOR USING THIS BOOK

Try to read the whole book through in one sitting. Just skim it, if that's all you have time to do.

Then write down the four steps so you'll be more likely to remember them:

- Recognize
- Choose
- Enact
- Disengage

These words may not be meaningful to you now, but once you master the Four-Step Program, you'll want to keep these cues handy.

During the next backtalk incident, apply the four steps immediately. Perhaps you'll stop the backtalk on the first application; perhaps you'll lose your nerve and give in. In any case, the hardest thing about using this book—taking immediate action — will have been initiated. You'll be on your way to establishing a *norm of communication* in your home.

WHAT THIS BOOK WILL NOT DO

Backtalk assumes your children are like Mary and John Jones's children: of normal intelligence, brought up to consider the feelings of others, and blessed with family members who, for the most part, behave well toward one another. This book will not tell you how to deal with neurologically impaired children, delinquent behavior, substance abuse, or physical attacks. This book will not diagnose or suggest cures for children who have psychiatric problems.

A note from Audrey Ricker: As a parent in the early 1960s who believed in progressiveness, I allowed my son to say anything he wanted whenever he wanted. By the time he was four, he had been expelled from the city's best nursery school for talking back to the teacher. Most frightening of all, he had begun to accompany his backtalk with acting-out behavior, such as throwing a chair across the room during an appointment with a psychologist. That doctor told me that my son was in a phase of self-expression that he would soon grow out of. But he was so completely out of hand that I was not sure he would ever get self-control on his own.

Though the psychologist told me I was risking psychological damage to my son, I allowed my new husband to discipline him verbally when he backtalked. Soon the boy not only became pleasant to live with but was able to attend a new preschool and make many more friends. I consider the stopping of my son's backtalk a turning point in his life. I'm sure he would not have gotten over it by himself, and I believe he would have landed in serious trouble with teachers, family, and friends.

PART ONE:

WHAT, WHY, WHEN, AND HOW

1.

FRANK TALK ABOUT BACKTALK

Case History #2: A twelve-year-old girl, Sandy, comes home from school and finds her mother in the home office, talking to a friend. The girl holds on to the doorknob, leans into the room without greeting either woman, and states, "I'm going over to Franny's." She's about to turn on her heel when Anne, the mother's friend, says, "Hi, Sandy."

The girl ignores Anne's greeting and says to her mother, ". . . and I might stay there for dinner."

The mother, slightly embarrassed for her daughter, says, "Be back early."

Sandy mutters, "Yeah, right," and exits the room, slamming the door.

Mom sums up this scene with a judgment she hopes will make both her and Sandy look better: "Adolescence!"

But the judgment doesn't work. The daughter *is* arrogant and bad-mannered, and her mother, hurt beneath the cavalier apology, is intimidated by trendy notions about letting children express themselves freely and being a "good parent."

Her friend feels foolish, wanting to defend Mother by saying something to defuse this girl's authority, but afraid to interfere. Above all, these women both feel a bit ashamed, temporarily immobilized because they have allowed Sandy's backtalk to render them powerless.

This case history is a good example of backtalk because it shows how tone, body language, and silence can be as much a part of backtalk as words, which in this case were limited to two brief sentences. The girl's announcement can be labeled as backtalk because it was inappropriate (Sandy was not being spoken to in a negative tone), hostile (she failed to acknowledge either her mother's friend or her mother), and uncooperative. Sandy's behavior was meant to control the conversation, not to initiate a dialogue about what she wanted to do.

This kind of unexpected backtalk is also meant to control the psychological mood of the home. Everyone in the family walks on eggshells to avoid saying something that will set Sandy off again.

THE BACKTALK-FREE HOME EXAMINED

The pleasures of the backtalk-free home are simple but profound. Sadie and Bessie Delaney, who wrote their best-selling memoir, *Having Our Say*, after they'd both reached the age of one hundred, talk about this kind of home in their book. All ten Delaney children had to speak respectfully to their parents and to one another. They could express themselves hon-

estly so long as they did so respectfully. As a result, the atmosphere in their home was happy, productive, and stimulating.
No one member, including either of the parents, had the right
to intimidate any other member verbally.

Respectful, backtalk-free interaction is illustrated in this
imaginary rewrite of Case History #2.

A twelve-year-old girl, Sandy, comes home from school
and finds her mother in the home office talking to a friend.
The girl holds on to the doorknob, leans into the room, and
greets both women.

Sandy: Hi, Mom. Hi, Anne.
Mom: Hi, Sandy, how was your day?
Sandy: Fine. I'm going over to Franny's, okay?
Mom: Yes, that's fine.
Anne: How's your algebra class? Still having problems?

All three discuss Sandy's new algebra tutor for a few minutes.

Sandy: Well, I should go. I told Franny I'd either call
her or come over by four-thirty. Oh, I may stay there
for dinner, if it's okay.
Mom: I'm sorry, darling, but Grandma's coming in at
eight, and you know how I hate driving to the airport
alone.
Sandy: (Sigh.) Okay. Can you pick me up at Franny's?
Mom: Sure. Be ready for me about six-thirty.

Sandy: If they eat early . . .

Mom: Fine, join them by all means. But you don't want to rush their dinner.

Sandy: No, but they usually eat around five-thirty.

Mom: If they don't, we'll get White Castle to go. (To her friend) Sandy's favorite is White Castle.

Anne: (Rolls her eyes and smiles.) So was mine at that age!

Sandy: I'm off. Bye, Mom. Bye, Anne.

If this scene sounds too idyllic and unrealistic, rest assured it is not. It shows the way respectful family members can interact and negotiate win-win situations for one another.

Why did Sandy behave so rudely in the first example? Because her goal was most likely to show her mother's friend who was boss in the house, to show her mother she would tolerate no discussion of her lifestyle, and to show them both that she would do as she pleased.

We are assuming in this book that you, as a proud parent, are basically caring, non-abusive, and genuinely desirous of a household in which respectful behavior by all members is the norm. We are also assuming that backtalk is never justified. We believe that allowing the child to continue it is a disservice to the child because it prevents her from learning more effective social strategies that will enable her to have a much happier, more productive life.

REASONS FOR BACKTALK

The reason why every child will *try* backtalk is a natural one: the child is looking for ways to have significance and will often try to find a place in the home through power-seeking and attention-getting behavior.

Another reason for backtalk is that parents sometimes model backtalk for their children by speaking rudely to spouses, family, or friends and by using brutal remarks and sarcasm in an attempt to control their children's behavior.

Other contributors to the backtalk epidemic are the mainstream media—television, film, video games, and popular music. This topic will be dealt with in more detail in Chapter 10. For now, parents must understand that the popular media not only encourage backtalk but reward it with laughter from other characters and stardom for the actor. Though perhaps justified by the evil adult characters, the message of these episodes is that backtalk gets a child lots of terrific attention, brings adults under the child's control, and is almost never punished, at least not by post–Cliff and Clair Huxtable type parents.

A fourth reason for rampant backtalk is the influence of progressive child-rearing experts and educators. This movement started with Dr. Spock in the late 1950s and picked up strength in the 1960s with progressive education in the public schools. By the 1970s, children could do no wrong in school. Everything from bad behavior to bad grades was considered the fault of poor teaching or the inability of teachers to relate to the students.

The progressive child-rearing movement has also contributed to the fifth reason for wholesale backtalk—the
power of the peer culture. Emboldened by their freedom to do
and say whatever they wished, children years ago began using
friends, instead of adults, as models to emulate.

Not that these developments are *all* bad. Beaver Cleaver
was certainly a lot less amusing than Darlene Conner on
Roseanne. Education was a lot more boring and repressive
before the progressives. Many pre–Dr. Spock child-rearing
experts did advocate harsh, if not sadistic, rules—such as
substituting the bottle for the breast and ignoring crying
infants. But now progressive beliefs work together to sanction
and encourage backtalk in ways that are unprecedented.

Will forbidding backtalk, or curbing a "fresh mouth,"
hurt a child? At least one very successful person says no. As a
rebellious fourteen-year-old who had just gone to live with
her natural father, Oprah Winfrey was forbidden to address
him as "Pops." This household rule and others did not hurt
her, she claims. Because of her father, she says, "I believe I am
where I am today."

Prohibiting backtalk won't hurt if it's done properly—
with respect and without focusing unduly on the backtalker.
The methods outlined in this book will accomplish these goals
and, at the same time, teach respect and social interaction.
Other benefits include clarity and improved communication
among all members of the household.

2.

THE FOUR-STEP
PROGRAM FOR DEALING
WITH BACKTALK

We've created the following simple steps for reacting to back-talk.

Step 1. The first step is to *recognize* the backtalk. Here's the best test: if it hurts you, embarrasses you, annoys you, or leaves you feeling helpless, it's backtalk.

Step 2. The second step is to *choose* the right consequence for the behavior. You should do this ahead of time. In the case of Sandy, the twelve-year-old in Case History #2, a good consequence would have been that she not be allowed to go to her friend's house. Any backtalk or rude behavior automatically means that the child will not do what she wants or has planned to do—such as go to soccer practice or to a dance lesson.

Step 3. The third step is to *enact* the consequence. The mother must *tell* Sandy she cannot go to her friend's house. In a calm voice she should say that the girl's behavior amounts to backtalk; that it is taking Mother's time, energy, and goodwill in her efforts to deal with it; that it is not acceptable; and that Sandy will not be going to Franny's house that day. If Sandy reacts badly to this statement, which she undoubtedly will, then the mother should proceed to Step 4.

Step 4. The fourth step is to *disengage* from a struggle with the backtalker. The mother should initially ignore the bad behavior and continue to talk with her friend. If the child's behavior continues, the mother should calmly excuse herself from the visiting friend, take the loudly protesting child to her room, and leave the child alone, thus disengaging herself from Sandy's fierce struggle to get the mother to change her mind.

These four steps may sound easy to implement, and for some parents they will be. But for the overindulgent parent, they will be challenging and will take lots of determination, practice, and self-control. One difficulty is that contemporary parents want to be good buddies with their children instead of teachers, leaders, and guides. They have a hard time understanding that their children sometimes will not act like good friends but will occasionally be typical young people trying out types of behavior that are not acceptable.

Yes, you can and should use the four steps immediately if your child starts backtalking. Change is much easier to put into effect if the justifications and methods are well understood. Here is a thorough explanation of each of the four steps.

STEP 1. *RECOGNIZING* Backtalk

Recognizing backtalk means more than simply identifying it. It means acknowledging backtalk as a form of communication you don't like. This communication can consist of no words (rolling the eyes and sighing), few words (as in Sandy's "Yeah, right," or the ever-popular "Whatever"), or an extended diatribe that gathers intensity as it goes along.

The hardest part of Step 1 is accepting your assessment of the child's communication. You can be infuriated at the backtalk, even hurt to the point of speechlessness, and then feel incredibly stupid for feeling bad when your child says his backtalk was not meant to hurt. "I didn't mean anything," he might say with a suddenly innocent look. "You're just overreacting, Mom." Guilt-ridden by this time, some parents end up hugging the child and apologizing for overreacting. Then they promise never to overreact again.

Case History #3: When Amanda was a child, her mother was gone most of the time, working two jobs to help support her family when her father was laid off from his job. So Amanda made sure her own daughters got as much of her company as they wanted.

When her girls began telling her what was wrong with her, Amanda was touched. "They tell me not to chew with my mouth open," she would say. "Isn't that cute? And they let me know right away when I say something they think is 'just so stupid.'" What seemed like caring to Amanda, who was divorced by that time, eventually escalated until every word out of each daughter's mouth was a hurtful insult. Nothing she did could please the girls. Amanda's domination by her daughters increased exponentially until finally her friends planned a sort of intervention during which they told Amanda how unpleasant it was to visit her when her daughters were home. Only then did Amanda realize that what she regarded as her daughters' well-meaning advice was actually backtalk that hurt her very much.

Her solution was not to confront them but to encourage them to move in with other relatives because she could no longer handle them. This solution worked well for Amanda, who began dating and having a good time. But today, some ten years later, the girls are still drifting in and out of relationships, unable to hold a job or finish a degree program.

This case history shows how parents can choose to see backtalk as well-meaning advice because they don't want to see it for what it is.

Here are some other common examples of backtalk that are often unrecognized in the beginning. We've listed them in age categories.

Up to age three: (*Yes, backtalk starts that early!*) "Bad Mommy," "I don't like you," and "No!"
Age four to six: "I hate you," "Shut up," "That's mine, don't touch it," and "You can't make me." "As if!" is also gaining in popularity, according to some parents.
Age six to eight: "You're stupid!" or "I'm not doing that!"

Age eight to eleven: "Oh, give me a break!" "That sucks!" Plus a lot of eye-rolling and huffing and sighing. "All the other kids get to do it!"

Age twelve to fourteen: "Mom" (or Dad), "you know absolutely nothing about music" (or video games or clothes or anything else the child cares about). "You have to take me to the mall" (or do anything else the child demands). "You call this edible?"

Age fifteen to seventeen: "Dad, you need help." "Don't bother me!"

Age seventeen or older: "I'm stressed [tired, bummed out, overworked, etc.], okay?"

These age categories are meant to be flexible. The more precocious the child, the more likely he is to use advanced backtalk. The less verbal a child is, the more she's likely to stay in the "You're stupid" and "You can't make me" stages.

We know it's risky to suggest that the "terrible twos" should be limited in any way. Many child development experts believe two-year-olds are expected to backtalk as part of their growth process. We believe that children of this age are capable of learning and should be taught what speech they can and cannot use. We deal more with age-related backtalk later on.

The content of these messages is not important—the tone and attitude are. Like darts dipped in poison, these messages and others like them are meant to immobilize the target instantly. The receiver of these comments feels humiliated, angry, and paralyzed with guilt, all at the same time. The parent can't figure out what to do, and so does nothing or uses the same tactics on the child.

Many backtalk recipients are so glad when the backtalkers do let them alone, even temporarily, that they act grateful, not angry, and never refer to the incident again. Those who react with anger bring more angry backtalk their way, which starts a cycle that ends only when one participant or the other gets exhausted or leaves the room.

Recognizing backtalk is done in part by identifying the feelings the backtalk causes. Sometimes, however, things children say cause discomfort or sadness but cannot be classified as backtalk.

▲ ■ ●

HERE IS AN EXAMPLE OF GENUINE COMMUNICATION FROM A CHILD THAT SHOULD NOT BE MISTAKEN FOR BACKTALK:

Troy was the six-year-old son of Enid, a working mother who was so busy she often went weeks without exchanging more than a few words a day with him. Once, while Enid was listening to her Japanese-language-lesson audiotape as she drove him to karate class, he said, "Mommy, I think you're bored with me." Enid was cut to the quick by this response, because it made her realize how she was treating Troy. But in no sense could this sad statement be considered backtalk. It was meant not to control but to clarify the child's perception of his mother's behavior. From that moment on, Enid made a point of completely focusing on Troy for at least an hour a day.

Here are some other things we've known children to say that caused discomfort but were not backtalk:

"Mommy, why are you mad all the time?"
"Grandpa, please don't yell at my mother."
"Dad, I don't like it when you don't go places with Mom and me."
"I wish we had a nicer house to live in like Billy does."
"I really would rather not wear clothes from yard sales no matter how new they look, because I don't feel good in them."

These examples of honest communication from children, spoken in a matter-of-fact voice rather than in a whining, mean, or sarcastic tone, need to be listened to, validated, and discussed, not dismissed as backtalk.

▲ ■ ●

STEP 2. *CHOOSING* a Consequence

A consequence used to stop the backtalk cannot be delayed and must be logical. To understand this step, pretend you are about thirteen years old. You are eating dinner with your family, and you ask, "Is this stuff supposed to be edible?" You are told that such talk is not acceptable and that as a result you will leave the table immediately and will not be going to the Dairy Queen with the family after dinner. Both consequences are logical results of your refusing to communicate in the manner your parents require at family gatherings. You will not get to eat the dinner, communicate with the family, and share in their more pleasurable activities. Any pleas on your part that you are hungry will be ignored.

What follows is an actual case history showing a choice of logical consequence that is so simple, it is elegant.

Case History #4: Susan, age eight, was spending the night at a friend's house. This was the first time she had stayed over with Becky, whom her parents did not know particularly well. Susan's mother, June, worked with Becky's mother at the insurance company where both were employed as executives.

At about nine that night, Becky told Susan to call her parents and tell them to bring over her VCR, since Becky's was not working. By that point, having been exposed to hours of Becky's nonstop backtalk to her own parents, Susan did not hesitate to demand that her parents drive the three or four miles to Becky's house immediately.

"But we're planning to use the VCR later," Susan's mother said.

"I need that VCR now!" Susan replied imperiously. "You can watch your movie tomorrow." She then rolled her eyes for Becky's benefit. "Oh, Mom! I mean, what is the big deal? You just get up, get in the car, and get over here!"

June knew exactly what consequence was most logical in this case. "We will be right over, Susan," she said crisply. "You be dressed and ready to come home."

"I don't think so," Susan said in a perfect imitation of Becky's tone when Becky used those words earlier as a back-talk response.

"The tone you have just used to me and the way you spoke to me were disrespectful. Your behavior is not acceptable."

"I don't believe this," Susan shrieked. "I'm not coming home now, I don't care what you say."

"Please tell Becky's mother you will be leaving shortly," said June, ignoring Susan's tone. "Be packed and ready to go in half an hour."

"Becky wants to talk to you," Susan began, but June quickly ended the call. Within half an hour, she and her husband were at Becky's door. Susan was not packed and had not told anyone she was being picked up. June and her husband told Becky and Becky's parents what they were doing and why. The parents chatted pleasantly, ignoring the tension as Susan prepared to go home.

Susan never tried such backtalk again in any situation, June reported. The consequence of having to come home was very logical because it was directly related to the backtalk.

Here is another example of a logical consequence chosen in a teaching situation.

Case History #5: Shelley worked at a summer camp, teaching kids how to create their own computer video games. Among her twenty students was Kevin, a very bright four-teen-year-old video game and computer expert who made the class impossible for her to teach with his sarcastic comments. Constantly, he spoke out in class, refused to do any assigned work, and encouraged others to slack off. "His main complaint was that we didn't have enough computers to work on. I was disappointed about that too, but there was no money in our budget for additional computers," Shelley explained. "So I taught preproduction, script writing, and other activities that could be done with pencil and paper—the main supplies we had. All the other kids adjusted well to this limitation until Kevin informed them that it was too much like 'real school' and they shouldn't put up with it because this camp was supposed to be fun." Shelley endured Kevin's behavior, often ending up screaming at him like a shrew.

After learning of the Four-Step Program, Shelley got an opportunity to try it out on Kevin the day after a field trip to a video game production company. "Kevin loved the field trip and behaved very well while he was on it. But the day afterward he was awful in class again. I made the announcement that the video game producer wanted the names of students I felt would be good at testing video games. Of course, Kevin shouted out that I'd better give the producer his name."

Shelley suddenly realized the most logical consequence for Kevin and for the other students influenced by him. "No, Kevin," Shelley said. "You've continued to make the class difficult for me after you were told what rules to follow. I could not give you a referral to anyone." Kevin's reaction? "He screamed," Shelley said. "He literally screamed for five whole minutes at the top of his lungs.

"Then he said I couldn't treat him like that. I did not respond. He screamed again, but most of the kids paid no attention to him. Then he said, 'Just who do you think you are? You have no right to treat me like this.'"

Shelley responded to this backtalk with another logical consequence—having Kevin removed from the classroom for the rest of that day. When he came back the next day, Kevin asked Shelley if she would change her mind about referring him to the video game producer if he was "real good." Loudly, so all the class could hear, Shelley said, "No, I am not changing my mind." Kevin then sighed and, for the first time since camp started, began working on illustrations with his group. He was fine for the rest of the class period.

"I honestly believe," Shelley added, amazed, "that this was the first time Kevin had actually had to face a consequence of his behavior. He was so surprised. So were the other children."

Shelley's choice of consequence was very logical. No one can be expected to give a good reference to someone who has treated her badly. Shelley was sorry that she could not have used the Four-Step Program the first time Kevin disrupted class. "I should have chosen a logical consequence immediately," Shelley said. "Next time I'll know."

STEP 3. *ENACTING* the Consequence

To be effective, a consequence of backtalk must be *immediate* as well as logical. After choosing the most logical consequence, the parent (or other adult authority) must enact the consequence immediately, without giving the backtalker another chance, no matter how much she pleads and promises to change.

In the case of Susan talking back to her parents from a friend's house, the logical consequence of the backtalk was enacted immediately—the daughter was brought home. It wasn't easy to do, but the parents had prepared themselves for this step.

Shelley, the teacher, admitted that immediate enactment was very hard. "I'd been so used to threatening 'One more time and I'll . . .' and to believing that a child's promise to be good from now on was valid that I had to force myself to enact the consequence right then and there."

Shelley added that it was especially difficult to avoid the word "if." "It seemed so natural to tell Kevin, '*If* you treat me badly one more day, I won't refer you as a game tester.' Or 'I'll refer you *if* you're good today.' I never realized how much teachers rely on threats and 'ifs.'" Yet "if" is a bargaining word, and bargaining with a child is futile for three reasons:

1. It gives him choices. In the case of backtalk, the child should have no choice about displaying the behavior. It is unacceptable, period.

2. Bargaining puts the child in charge by empowering him as a negotiator. He is not in charge in the backtalk situation; the adult is.

3. Bargaining buys the backtalker invaluable time. By saying, "If you continue to use that tone, you won't go anywhere this weekend," you invite the child to prolong the backtalk (she knows she can negotiate again when the weekend comes) and postpone consequences for a few days. For the parent, the "if" clause means fulfilling the ultimatum later, when neither the parent nor the child can really remember the original backtalk. All the original bad feelings may have to be dredged up again by the parent so she will have the motivation necessary to enact the consequence.

A much better solution is to enact the consequences for the backtalk *immediately,* as the following case history shows.

Case History #6: Shelley was able to enact the first three steps when she taught a class in beginning filmmaking. "The kids had to get in groups, and each group had to come up with a proposal for a two-minute movie with a beginning, a middle, and an end. Three of the girls in one group came to me and said the fourth girl in their group, Joan, would not listen to their ideas. They said that Joan insisted, using very rude backtalk, that they use her ideas.

"When I spoke to Joan, she complained that the other three were 'bad' because they refused to listen to *her!* I told Joan the other girls did not like the way she spoke to them. Joan replied that they deserved to be spoken to rudely because they would not let her have her way. Without batting an eye, I chose and enacted the most logical consequence. I informed Joan that she would work alone. The other three could form their own group without her.

"Well, Joan was furious—she fully expected me to make the other girls follow her lead. When she saw I wasn't changing my mind, she said I should give her another chance to get along with the girls. The hardest part came when Joan changed from rudeness to tears. How could I be so mean? she sobbed. Didn't I know she had a genuine learning disability? But I knew better than to give in. I told her she could 'hire' (request) other students to help her with acting, props, and camera work and that they could decide whether to work for her or not. If they did work for her, she would be the boss. But she would be the only member of her group. It all worked out so well! Joan enjoyed being producer, director, writer, and star. She had no trouble finding 'employees' because many of the other students wanted more production experience than they were getting in their own groups. They realized that as 'employees' they had to do what Joan said. But Joan realized she had to treat them with kindness and fairness or they would quit. So she learned how to treat others to win their cooperation. She'll probably be a famous, powerful Hollywood producer someday."

Amanda, the mother of the two backtalking girls, followed step 1 by recognizing the backtalk. But the consequence she enacted — sending the children to live with other people — could not be called logical and was, in fact, an abdication of her parenting role and an acknowledgment of defeat. Thus, it never actually worked.

Whenever the girls returned home to visit Amanda, their treatment of their mother, though loving and pleasant at first, would soon deteriorate into backtalk that would escalate in rudeness and loudness until Amanda would send them away again, days before their visit was scheduled to end. Ironically, one of the girls once revealed during a heated backtalk attack that they would never dare talk to the relatives they lived with the way they spoke to their mother. They respected the relatives too much!

Here are some important points to keep in mind when you are responding to backtalk and preparing to enact a consequence:

- Talk only about your thoughts or feelings, not about what the child is doing or saying wrong. For example, you might say, in a neutral, matter-of-fact tone, "I find that kind of speech disrespectful and it makes me feel bad, so I've decided not to take you to Suzy's." Don't say, "You're a smart-mouthed brat and you're not going anywhere today!"

- Use respectful, *non-vengeful* words and tone even if the child does not. Say, for example, "I find that word offensive," instead of "Don't you ever say that filthy word to me again."

- State the consequence only once: "I felt mistreated when you called me that name. I feel hurt. I'm not willing to buy you those new shoes this evening." Do not justify or explain your decision. Kids know what's logical and what's not, even though they may try to convince you otherwise.

- Link the consequence to the offense. For example, point out to the child once that whatever activity comes immediately after backtalk will be withdrawn as a consequence: "Because you called me stupid when I asked you to pick up your toys, I'm taking those toys away from you for a while." Don't spank the child or say, "You bad girl, you better not call me that again!"

- When the child begs for another chance—as in "If you'll just buy me those shoes tonight so I can wear them to Jimmy's party tomorrow, I promise I won't ever, ever say that again!"—don't give in to her. The only way to win credibility is to follow through. Yes, following through will sometimes hurt both of you, but it's part of your job as parent.

- Do use your feelings as a reason for consequences. Do say, "I feel hurt," "I feel bad," "I feel angry," "I feel helpless," as a reason for imposing a consequence. You have a right not to want to do good things for someone who is treating you badly. Just be matter-of-fact, never vengeful in your use of consequences. Any of these examples could be vengeful if said in an "I'll get you!" tone of voice.

▲ ■ ●

DO'S AND DON'TS FOR RESPONDING TO BACKTALK

Things you should never say in responding to backtalk:

- "What did you say?" The child will almost always reply, "Nothing." You will respond, "I heard what you said." The child will again deny that he said anything. An argument will ensue, during which the child will be in charge.
- "I heard what you said." The child will

respond with some remark such as "Whatever!" or "What? What did I say?" and end up in charge.

- "Now you're in trouble!" The child will respond with, "What did *I* say?" in an innocent tone. You will repeat what he said. He will insist he did not mean it "that way," and he'll end up in charge.

Things you should always say when responding to backtalk:

- "That kind of talk (or behavior) makes me feel hurt (or tired or however it makes you feel). Therefore, I'm not going to . . ." You identify the behavior, you identify the effect of the behavior, and you stay in charge of the situation.
- "That kind of talk is unacceptable in our house (or our family or my house or to me). Therefore I'm going to . . ." You establish the norms of communication.
- "I do not allow that tone of voice (such as sarcasm or whining) or those gestures (such as eye rolling)." You make your position clear.

(More ideas for choosing and enacting consequences will be found in Chapter 5, the workbook chapter.)

STEP 4. *DISENGAGING* from the Struggle

As you've seen in many of the case histories, a struggle often ensues when the first three steps are initially implemented. Only Amanda avoided this struggle by putting her daughters out of her house. She thus missed step 4—disengaging from their fury while they were acting it out. Step 4 is crucial because children must see that no matter what *they* may do, Mom or Dad is done with the incident and has calmly gone on with life. Pretty soon the child tires of acting out the fury. Eventually the child will give up the behavior—the back-talk—which caused the consequences that made her furious.

Here is another way to think of step 4: The parent, by disengaging from the struggle, is showing a lack of interest in the protest behavior. As a result the child understands that this behavior will not get him his way or the attention, power, and revenge that add up to the misguided sense of belonging and importance he wants.

In case history #2, the mother could have disengaged by taking Sandy to her room. If the child is too old or too big to be physically removed, we recommend that the parent leave the room and tend to something else. The point is, do not argue or entertain discussion or attempt to stop the pleading and protests.

MORE WAYS TO DISENGAGE

Take a book with you on all excursions. If you have to remove a backtalking child from a museum or a theater and then wait for the rest of your family or friends to finish their outing, you'll have something to read while you wait with the child in the car, so you will not be drawn into an argument or a temper tantrum. If you can't concentrate on a book while the child is with you, take along some paperwork, a few letters to answer, or a diary to write in.

Sitters for those times when you need to disengage yourself from the backtalker should be mature adults who are reliable but not necessarily popular with your children, and who can be counted on to adhere to a structured schedule. They should not be young teens who may be more fun for your child to be with than you are!

The point is to remove yourself after enacting the consequence and not to show any response to the child in your body language or your voice and facial expressions. The child will soon quit, because the action is no longer getting the negative-attention responses from you he wants—hurt, anger, helplessness and irritation—in order to feel misguided importance.

In Part Two we'll explain in more detail how to implement the Four-Step Program.

3.

WHAT'S HARDEST ABOUT
USING THIS PROGRAM

Learning to recognize backtalk is usually simple. The third
step, *enacting* the consequences, tends to be the most difficult
for parents. Enactment needs to be done immediately, with no
opportunity for a second chance and no consideration of
promises to "be good" or "never talk like that again." Most
children find this lack of a second chance infuriating,
unthinkable, and a true violation of their rights.

So why not give them a second chance?

The main reason is that taking action immediately gets
the incident over with immediately.

Reason two is that second chances—as in "If you do that
one more time, I will . . ."—often turn out to be idle threats.
The parent may not mean these threats to be idle, but often
lacks the energy or time or anger to follow through if the child
talks back "one more time"—and the child probably will, just
to test the parent.

Reason three is that second chances can also cause over-
reactions. Knowing that he or she *must* act when the child

talks back a second time, the parent may work up too much rage and seem to be out of control. The fact that the child actually does try the backtalk a second time can cause the parent to get much angrier than she would get under normal circumstances.

Reason four is that giving the child a second chance puts him in charge. It allows him to decide if he will backtalk again, and this gives him power over the entire family's mood. A simple relapse and everyone's overpowered and upset—what a heady feeling of power for the child!

In short, children must know that every time they talk back they'll have to face consequences—starting as soon as they begin the backtalk!

But you may still feel that you're being a dictator, because many child-rearing books, counselors, and other experts—not to mention your child and other family members—try to make you feel like a dictator. These "experts" subscribe to a so-called progressive school of thought where the parent is the friend.

What you and these others need to realize is that it is your job to set the emotional tone and provide discipline and guidance to children in your household. It is your job to provide them with a way to feel important and a sense of belonging in the family. You must teach them the type of behavior that will enable them to belong positively in your household. This is not done by giving them a second chance whenever they misbehave. It is done by providing logical consequences for behavior that is unacceptable to the household.

If you still need to be convinced that you should not give second chances for backtalk, here is an excellent reason why: By giving your child a second chance you teach him that he should expect others—teachers, spouses, friends, employers, for instance—to give him a second, third, and fourth chance on demand. He will have to learn how backtalk affects people. If he never learns how people feel about what he says, he will not develop empathy for others. Children who lack empathy for others also lack respect for others, and so they fail to develop the positive sense of belonging they need for satisfaction in life.

We know it's hard to enact consequences immediately. It's not *you*—the kind, loving, forgiving parent who always gives in; the soft touch who can always be manipulated by her child to do what the child wants. Enacting immediate consequences takes backbone, thought, and courage that you may not feel at the moment.

It may help to know that, in later life, adult children speak well, even admiringly, of parents who set limits.

The next case history—a true story told by Audrey Ricker—demonstrates all four steps of the Four-Step Program for backtalk.

Case History #7: I will never forget the anguish I suffered when my new husband actually enacted consequences on my son for backtalking. When Noah informed his new stepfather in the same sarcastic tone he used with me that "I don't help with dishes, and you can't make me do anything I don't want," my husband acted immediately. He told Noah to do the dishes alone. He told him to get into the kitchen and not come out until the dishes were done. My son screamed and looked at me. I knew this was the first moment of the rest of our lives, so *I looked away.* This was the first time in Noah's life that anyone had made him do anything against his will. By looking away, I was betraying not just my son but also A. S. Neill, founder of the progressive school Summerhill; Dr. Spock, who believed parents should always be best friends with their kids; my son's psychologist, who believed Noah's backtalk was a healthy expression of deeply repressed feelings; and my mother, who had taught me that this beautiful male child could do no wrong and should always be indulged. I was sure I was creating an ax murderer, a serial killer, a ne'er-do-well, or a delinquent.

Disengaging from that struggle was almost unbearably difficult. I sat in the living room, trying to read while my husband watched television. I was sure my son would break every dish in the kitchen. Every five minutes I had to stop myself from going in to check on him. But in half an hour or so he came out and said casually that the dishes were done. From then on, the dishes were his job in the family. My son never again talked back to my husband—or to me, either, for that matter.

I am not going to say we all lived happily all the time after that. I *will* say that in that moment I learned that actions speak louder than words.

PART TWO:

PRACTICE

4.

IMPLEMENTING THE FOUR-STEP PROGRAM

As we've established, the Four-Step Program outlined in this book can be put to use immediately, the next time backtalk occurs. But taking something away—in this case, the power to backtalk—works better if there is a desired positive experience to replace it. One of these desired experiences can be ongoing life in a backtalk-free home.

THE BACKTALK-FREE HOME

A backtalk-free home is one that reflects the love of one's family, the closeness family members feel for one another, the comforts of one another's company, and the good things about family life.

A backtalk-free home is a home that functions happily for *all* members. That home will be full of respect, encouragement, and kind words. If you do not know what such a home is like, we advise you to go shopping—that is, to visit the homes of others and make a mental note about what you like.

Certain movies and television shows also offer a positive representation of family interaction. Of course, some of these depictions of family life are highly idealized—it's unrealistic to hope that your family will always act like the characters in a Disney film. The idea here is simply to observe as many backtalk-free homes as possible.

You'll also find some movie and television families that are supposed to be happy cater to backtalking children. You'll find happy homes aren't necessarily occupied by nuclear families. The play *You Can't Take It With You,* for instance, is about a delightful extended family.

You can also read biographies. As described in *Love Can Build a Bridge,* Naomi Judd's family was, in her younger years, full of loving people. Her mother always made her children feel that she enjoyed having them around. The children were taught to respect all adults and one another, eccentrics included.

A *National Geographic* documentary on the Amazon rain forest shows that money is not necessary for a happy family. In the particular tribe examined in this documentary, the members all lived as one huge family, eating, sleeping, and living together twenty-four hours a day. When a young girl of this tribe married an American anthropologist and moved with him to New Jersey, she tried hard to adjust to a new life filled with everything other Americans want—two beautiful children, clothes, a gorgeous one-family home in a good neighborhood, charge accounts at all the best stores, a car of her own, immediate membership in her husband's intellectual social circle.

In less than five years, however, this woman was back in the rain forest with her "real" family, once again living almost naked in a lean-to, weaving vines and cooking fresh-killed game in handmade clay pots over an open fire. The charge accounts, stores, and malls meant nothing to her compared to the pleasures of being with her family in the rain forest. Why? Her explanation was simple: she was lonely in New Jersey, where just one family occupied a whole house. As the documentary ended, this woman was insisting that her ex-husband send their older daughter to her to be raised as she had been. This tribe had many rules of operation. For instance, starting fights was forbidden, and everyone had to do certain assigned chores. But the pleasure shared by its members in one another's company went on all their waking hours.

The constant family closeness in hunter-gatherer cultures precludes backtalk. This closeness would be difficult to accomplish in our culture, with all our materialistic values, our substance-abuse and physical abuse problems, and our other customs and beliefs that seem to discourage enjoyment by family members of one another's company. Despite these obstacles, however, family happiness is achievable with effort, practice, and planning ahead.

If you have a clear idea of how you want your family to

behave, you'll have an easier time dealing with backtalk. You will want to discourage any form of communication that disrupts this idea.

Once the idea is clear in your mind, decide which tones, speech forms, and gestures you don't want in your home. Sarcasm, eye rolling, nasty tones of voice, inappropriately hostile answers, unprovoked verbal attacks — you don't have to put up with any of these disruptions. Parents need to model respectful behavior with each other for their children's benefit. Adults in peaceful homes usually encourage and practice the following communication habits:

- Being glad to see any family member when he or she comes into a room.
- Saying hello or good-bye when an individual enters or leaves the house.
- Asking members questions about their day at school or work, or about recreational activities.
- Listening to the answers, hearing what is being said, commenting on the answers, following up with more questions or statements when the situation merits further discussion.

Here are some examples of homes in which negative forms of communication have taken over.

The Competitive Home. In this home, children must compete for attention by behaving in a way that is negative, powerful, and/or controlling, by saying or doing something that will get them more of their parents' attention than the other children get. By all accounts, Joe and Rose Kennedy's home was such a competitive home, with dinnertime being a contest for attention won by the child who behaved most aggressively.

The Silent Home. Here people seldom speak or eat together or in other ways interact. Sometimes family members are too exhausted to acknowledge one another. Sometimes they are too angry at what's going on in the outside world to be cheerful. And sometimes, having grown up in silent homes themselves, parents have no idea how to provide any other kind of environment.

The Cruel Home. Members of this kind of family use the home as a place to ventilate bad feelings. It's not that this home is abusive but rather that it is inundated with angry feelings that seem to poison the very air. People speak to one another rudely, if at all, stopping just short of meanness but seldom uttering a cheery word. Sometimes the anger in these homes is saved for one unlucky member. In her biography, Mary Tyler Moore implies that her childhood home was this way for her father, who was treated coldly by the women in her family.

The Nervous Home. If one or more adult authority figures has what are euphemistically called delicate nerves and indulges in outbursts of bad temper, tense sniffling episodes, or other unpleasant displays, most of the other household members will "catch" the delicate-nerves eruption as if it were a cold and either walk on eggshells or behave similarly. A simple "How are you?" is met with a suspicious "Why do you ask?" Everyone fears that the slightest wrong move will provoke an outburst. Such families are also said to be high-strung, tense, or, as Ali McGraw once described her family, "weird." Patti Davis, daughter of Ronald and Nancy Reagan, suggests that her childhood was spent in a nervous home.

All of these homes are shaped by the families' norms of communication. All breed backtalk among children, because all require the kind of hostility found in backtalk for belonging and gaining importance in a negative way. If your home is an extreme example of one of the models listed above, you may need help that extends beyond the scope of this book. Meanwhile, however, you can put energy into action instead of suffering.

PREPARING YOUR HOME TO BE A BACKTALK-FREE ZONE

How can you transform your home into a more positive environment for all members? There are many ways, but the main one is by deciding that adults are responsible for setting the mood and that this mood will be positive. Here are some ways to do this:

- Be at home as much as you can. Naomi Judd said

one thing she loved about her mother was that "she was always there."

- Be glad to see anyone who comes in. Give hugs, words of greeting, and big smiles to all who enter.

- Ask people how they are and how some project is going. Remember what they are involved in, so the questions can be individually tailored to the recipient's life.

- Recognize birthdays and other big days with special meals or small tokens of appreciation. Gifts can be simple and even funny—one mother we know has family members compete to see who can give the most outrageous yard-sale birthday gifts—just so they make the honored person feel special.

- Make dinner a big event. Give everyone a job to do in the preparation. If this isn't always possible on weeknights, plan ahead for special weekend meals.

- Make sure everyone contributes to the maintenance and operation of the home. Each person should have a real job that needs doing and that will be valued by others.

- Change any behavior that makes your home unhappy and that you are able to change—such as your children's backtalk. You needn't wait to start dealing with the backtalk. Institute the Four-Step Program immediately and keep at it. When one or both parents stay with the program for backtalk, they are in effect showing their respect for the home. They are taking the stand that this home from now on is to be valued and not abused and that participation in the family is a privilege. When the children see that parents mean business, they usually come to respect the family in ways that will make the home a happier place to be.

- Realize how much your family means to you. Think of all the pleasure every member has given you.

▲ ■ ●

GIVING CHILDREN A SENSE OF BELONGING

- Notice what children contribute to the household and any improvement they show in assigned chores. Say, for example, "You did a good job cleaning the house this morning. I appreciate your help!"
- Create huge colorful charts showing everyone's household job schedule.
- Allow children to check off each chore on the chart when they have completed it.

- Schedule regular family excursions such as trips to the ice cream parlor, the library, and museums.
- Have a family book club that assigns books everyone can read and discuss at regular meetings.
- Schedule family cooking lessons so all members can help with food preparation from an early age.
- Have children plan a month's worth of family excursions. Give them price and distance limits to work within.
- Have your family compile a video history as a Christmas project. Interview adult friends and family members about what they did for fun when they were children.
- Help your children organize used clothing and toy drives for children in shelters.

Most of these suggestions help create jobs for all family members. Others, such as excursions, contain built-in consequences—loss of that particular family pleasure as a result of backtalking.

▲ ■ ●

STRENGTHENING YOUR RESOLVE

Everyone you know will test your new position on backtalk. People will try to prevent this change by telling you the following:

- You have no right to change.
- You are fine just the way you are.
- You are overreacting to the backtalk.
- You have no right to impose your standards on your children.
- You are so cute when you get mad, but you just can't be taken seriously.

Other ploys will also be tried on you. Attitudes accompanying these attempts to prevent you from changing will range from gentle humor to rage. It will be your job to ignore them all! (More about how others will try to sabotage your backtalk position in Chapter 6.)

In all cases, stand up for yourself and what you believe. It may help if you remember a home is rather like the theater—you are the director and set designer, and you get to say what ambience will prevail. Of, if you prefer, you can think of your home as a restaurant where your aesthetic choices extend to the staff members' manners toward one another and customers. You choose what kind of mood prevails in your restaurant. Similarly, only you can decide the mood of your home, in a way that is conscious, clear, and premeditated.

ANNOUNCING YOUR CHANGES

If you feel it necessary, you can announce your stance on back-talk at a family meeting. But remember: your announcement is just that—an announcement, not a discussion. Make it quickly and clearly, and then go on to another subject. If you hate making announcements, just start dealing with backtalk on an incident-by-incident basis. After the third or fourth implementation of the Four-Step Program, children will get the idea. Before you realize that they've caught on, however, they will try to make you think you've gone crazy or that you have so violated their right to be themselves by your new policy that they are now submissive zombies with no reason to come alive again, oppressed servants who . . . You get the idea. They will, in short, try everything to make you feel guilty.

When this happens, you should adopt the following attitudes:

- Stay cheerful. Show no doubts.
- Have your consequences ready.
- Don't feel bad if your first attempts at the Four-Step program don't work. They will work sooner or later.
- Don't engage in anger, arguments, or explanation. Be respectful and kind but firm.

Record keeping—using the workbook, as described in Chapter 5—will make clear your goals and objectives for your home. It will remind you that you can have the mood of your home be what you want it to be.

LEARNING TO MANAGE SIBLING DYNAMICS

One or more of the following backtalk alliances may already exist among your children:

- An older or more dominant child may be setting the backtalk tone in your house.
- The youngest child of the family may be modeling backtalk because, unlike the other children, he's been allowed to get away with it.
- Two children could be cooperating to get you going emotionally.

Once the children see how you are now reacting to their backtalk, they may form new alliances. They might present themselves as a band of orphans ruled by a cold tyrant. They may gather together in cells of self-pity. They may act warmly toward the parent they perceive to be less firm on backtalk and show coldness to you. Or one child might secretly try to gain favor with you and turn on the others.

You need to recognize all of these alliances as power plays designed to get you under control. Children will try all kinds of political maneuvers. Keep using the Four-Step Program with all individuals, groups, and alliances.

DEALING WITH AGE DIFFERENCES

While the principles of the Four-Step Program remain the same for all children, these principles can produce different reactions from children of various ages. Your use of the Four-Step Program may vary slightly.

AGES THREE TO EIGHT

Before the age of three, children's speech tends to serve the function of boundary setting, individuation, and testing of the world. As such, it cannot be considered backtalk. But by the age of three, communication patterns are starting to form that need guidance. Children develop a strong need to belong in the family and so must learn the patterns of social behavior that will help them accomplish this goal in positive ways.

Recognizing Backtalk. The best rule of thumb is this: if the talk, tone, or gesture upsets you, it's backtalk. "You're a poopy, I hate you" from a four-year-old is no more acceptable than "You're a piece of s—t" from an eighteen-year-old.

Choosing a Consequence. For backtalkers in this age group, the best consequence is probably instant removal from family activities.

Enacting the Consequence. When the backtalk begins, you say cheerily, minimizing your emotional reaction, "That kind of talk (or behavior) is not acceptable in our family, Carl. Your behavior says that you don't want to be here with us. In twenty minutes perhaps you will change your mind and demonstrate that you want to be part of the group." You take Carl, screaming, to his room.

To other children who say, "He didn't mean anything," you reply, "Carl needs to learn what kind of speech is acceptable in our family. He's young and this is a good way to teach him." You then ignore the screams from Carl's room, plus sounds of banging and objects hitting walls. (The sound of glass breaking and the smell of smoke can be attended to, however.) Yes, you have to endure his misery, but the result will be well worth the price.

Disengaging from the Struggle. Once Carl is removed from the scene, you disregard his yelling from the bedroom and immediately find another activity to occupy your family's attention. Anything positive will do—discussing an upcoming birthday party, planning a weekend trip, making cookies, whatever will be positive, productive, and preclude focusing on Carl. The family needs to see that one of the consequences of backtalk is missing out on a rewarding experience.

AGES NINE TO ELEVEN

Recognizing the Backtalk. Backtalk in this age bracket is usually phrased so as to indicate that the backtalker has found you are not perfect:

"You are so uncool."

"You can't make me."

"Donny's mother keeps their house clean all the time by herself."

"Donny's mother makes lots of money. Why can't you, huh?"

Choosing a Consequence. You need to address the form of the backtalk, not its content. However painful that content may be, you must not dignify it with a denial ("I make lots of money, much more than Tom's mom, who doesn't even work!") or a defense ("If I weren't working to make money, I would keep the house clean.")

You need to take something away, remove a long-anticipated privilege, or refuse to grant an expected favor. Just be sure that the consequence is logically connected in some way to the backtalk: "That kind of tone and those kinds of words are not respectful, John. As a result, I feel less willing to spend time and energy doing what you want. I have decided not to drive you to Joey's tonight. I'm calling his mother now to cancel." This *must not* be said in a vengeful tone but matter-of-factly. Starting a tit-for-tat will only teach your child about getting even. The fact is that disrespect is hurtful—you don't show it and you won't accept it from others. Therefore, you are disinclined to be gracious to the child at that moment, and you are unwilling to do anything *for* the child.

Enacting the Consequence. As John shrieks, you must call Joey's mother. Tell her John's behavior has not been respectful, and so he cannot visit Joey. When John escalates his rage, go to step 4 and remove him from the room.

Disengaging from the Struggle. As John continues to protest from his room, begin talking to your family about interesting upcoming activities, or do something by yourself—take a walk, rake the yard, or read a book.

AGES TWELVE TO FOURTEEN

Recognizing the Backtalk. Teenagers have realized not only that you are not perfect but also that you are ridiculous. Backtalk from adolescents often includes shaming statements. "You don't know anything," or "You have no idea how to dress" or apply makeup, buy a car, or work out. You are told you have been judged and found inept.

Choosing a Consequence. The best consequence is one that is logical and consists of an action the teenager believes you will never dare take. In case history #1 (in the Introduction), for instance, the teenager backtalked his mother—"Can't you see I'm watching the show? God!"—when she asked him how he wanted his hamburger cooked. A logical consequence would have been for the mother to tell Joe that his tone was not acceptable and then do the unthinkable—leave him out of dinner.

Enacting a Consequence. No quarter must be given. Joe's failure to tell his mother how to fix his hamburger results in his not getting a hamburger. Many mothers would stand and seethe until Joe deigned to say "rare" or "medium" or "I don't care." Then they would fix Joe's hamburger—teaching the other children how to backtalk Mother just for the fun of it and to show who's in charge.

Disengaging from the Struggle. As stated, the fourth step involves getting on with your life while the backtalker continues protesting. But do you have a life worth getting on with? When you have older adolescents, having a good life of your own is especially important. Nothing impresses them more. The trick here is to be a dedicated parent—but *not* a doormat with no other purpose than seeing to the happiness of your offspring. The more quickly you appear to divert your interest from the backtalker to another topic in your life, the more subdued your backtalking adolescent will be. If there's anything your adolescent cares about, it's someone else's life—particularly one in which she may not be included.

AGES FIFTEEN TO TWENTY

Recognizing the Backtalk. Simple surliness tends to be the type of backtalk practiced by this age group. It's not chic among their peers to speak politely to parents. Grunts and snorts, the making of strange sounds with mouths full (which is often the case), or deliberate silence substitute for civil answers. Insisting on actual words from the child may elicit a pouting "Will you give me a break?" or "Can't you see I'm busy?" or "I don't *need* this! Jeez!" All this whining amounts to backtalk of the most insidious and annoying sort.

Choosing the Consequence. Teens this age are particularly difficult because they are by now used to getting their way with no consequences. If you're just starting to deal with their backtalk, think of all the things you provide that they need— housing, food, caring, nurturing, television, computer, clean sheets, and whatever else you can think of. Keep two facts firmly planted in mind: that you provide these benefits because you are able and want to; and that it's your home. Tell the child once that his backtalk is using up your energy and time. Before he can say, "That sounds like a personal problem to me," or something equally insolent, add that you won't use your energy and time doing something he wants—such as picking up his saxophone from the repair shop or having his new girlfriend to dinner.

Enacting the Consequence. Do not pick up the saxophone. Do tell him to inform his new girlfriend that the dinner invitation has been canceled. Make a quick list of other things you planned to do for him or give him so you'll have more consequences, if necessary.

Disengaging from the Struggle. Disregard his protestations that nothing in your life could be worth more time and energy than your child, no matter how that child acts. It's best when dealing with this age bracket to keep talking about your life beyond backtalk. Let the teen know what you're doing and enjoying. Continue to model the kind of communication you want from your almost grown child.

Don't take a different approach with girls than you do with boys. Backtalk is backtalk no matter what.

5.

WORKBOOK

If you keep a workbook, you will essentially write your own personalized book on backtalk. You'll be able to track your applications of the Four-Step Program, your feelings about its effectiveness, your list of consequences that got results and those that did not, the kinds of backtalk your children try and the resources you choose—people you can call and books you can read, if desired.

Of course, you can implement the backtalk program without keeping a workbook, but you'll react more consistently and feel more in control if you do.

Before continuing with this chapter, however, it is necessary to raise a red flag.

Warning: This notebook is for backtalk only! Do not record your feelings about, or dealings with, your children's pet neglect, sibling torture, or wall crayoning, even if this behavior seems related to the backtalk.

Why not? Primarily because the elimination of backtalk often eliminates other unacceptable types of behavior as well. And, secondarily, it is far better to deal with one kind of behavior thoroughly than with two or more less thoroughly.

HOW TO SET UP THE WORKBOOK

Any notebook with blank pages is fine, but it should allow for addition of pages as necessary.

Decide on a regular time for writing in the notebook—in the evening after the children are in bed if you're a night person, or in the morning before they get up or after they go off to school if you're more alert in the morning.

You can also write in the notebook on an ad hoc basis, recording progress as it occurs, consequences as you think of them, and resources when you discover them. However, keep your daily workbook time consistent if at all possible.

Date every entry you make. This is a habit you will find invaluable when you read your entries days or weeks later. "Did I feel that bad back then?" you'll think. "Goodness, how things have changed." But if the previous entry is undated, you won't know when "back then" actually was.

STARTING THE WORKBOOK

Be sure you list the following components of responding to backtalk:

1. Briefly describe *what happened* during the backtalk incident, how you felt, and why.
2. List what you did for a *consequence*, including your tone of voice, in reaction to the backtalk.

3. Describe what you did to *disengage* from any reaction to the consequence.

4. Describe *what happened after the disengagement* and what you did in response.

5. *Evaluate* the entire process, including what you would have done differently.

This sample entry illustrates what we mean:
1/13:

1. **What happened.** When I picked up my son after school, I asked him about his day. Chucky answered sarcastically, "You always ask me that. Get a life, Mom." I felt hurt and put down because I want so much for us to be able to talk pleasantly with each other.

2. **Consequence.** I told Chucky that I felt hurt and tired by his comment and therefore would not use time and energy later to drive him to band practice. I said it matter-of-factly.

3. **Disengagement.** When Chucky looked at me in disbelief, I turned on the radio and began singing along softly, ignoring his looks.

4. **What happened after the disengagement.** Chucky explained in a nice tone that he had to go to band practice tonight because he had to work on his solo. I said that maybe he could practice it tomorrow at school.

5. **Evaluation.** I ignored Chucky's attempts to get me

to change my mind, although he was polite. It worked! I didn't justify my decision or argue back. I did it right!

Here is another example:
1/15:

Backtalk recognized: As soon as I got home from work, Cary told me there was no Crystal Lite in the house and demanded to know why I hadn't remembered to buy it when she specifically asked me to. Without pausing she then demanded to know how she could be expected to stay on her diet without Crystal Lite. She said all this in a snide voice, rolling her eyes and shrugging her shoulders. The whole speech was backtalk. I felt irritated because of her mistreatment.

Consequence: I decided not to take her to the mall after dinner to meet her friend Annie. I told her, "Cary, your speech has conveyed disrespect. When I feel disrespected, I find my energy getting used up. Since you have used up my energy, I won't be driving you to the mall as we had planned. I'm tired."

Disengagement: I ignored Cary's screams. She literally screamed. I told her that if she continued screaming I would get up and go do gardening on the patio. She stopped screaming but was noticeably stony and sulky all during dinner. I ignored this behavior.

What happened after the disengagement: Cary ate a

little, did her dishwashing chore, and then went to her room and did homework. Then she asked me if I'd change my mind about driving her to the mall. I told her I would not change my mind. Then I went and turned on the television. Cary did not ask me again. Instead, she called Annie and said she could not meet her at the mall.

Evaluation: The consequence was appropriate. I have little energy when I come home from work and don't want to use that little bit coping with feelings of being disrespected. I did pretty well disengaging from Cary's struggle after enacting the consequence. I wish I had not given Cary a choice as to whether to stop screaming or have me go outside. I should have left as soon as she started screaming. I will not use the word "if" anymore.

KEEP A CONSEQUENCE LIST

In another section, list all the consequences you think of when they occur to you, so you'll have them ready when you need them. You might want to carry a small notebook in your purse for jotting down consequence ideas during the day. You can transfer them to your workbook when you make your regular daily entry.

Remember that the best consequences involve things you do for your children that take your time, energy, and money.

A word of warning: Don't worry if the consequences curtail activities you think are necessary for your children's enrichment. Such activities are privileges, not rights or obligations the parents owe the children.

The problem is that Chucky knows you want band for him as much as he wants it for himself. Thus, he thinks he can treat you disrespectfully without jeopardizing his band activities.

This assumption is not healthy either for you or for Chucky. He needs to learn that respectful behavior toward you comes before activities that may benefit him. *Do* use transportation to band practice and other time- and money-consuming efforts on your part in your consequences. You can also use cheerleading, ballet, sports, and all the other extracurricular activities that take so much of your time and energy.

While wholesome, productive, and life-enhancing, such activities must be considered a privilege your children earn. Otherwise, you'll be held hostage for the rest of their years with you. Even worse, they'll be able to use quitting these activities as a threat to you if you don't do what *they* want.

The main thing to remember about consequences is that the consequence must be logically connected to the backtalk. If the backtalk uses up your resources—your time, energy, and money—then you do not have time, energy, or resources left for something your children want and expect. Consequences happen as a matter of fact—not out of revenge on your part.

Also, remember that logical consequences should be enacted immediately and should be brief in duration. To decide you will not drive Chucky to band practice tonight is a logical consequence because Chucky talked back to you. But to say you will not drive him for a week would not be a logical consequence. It would be arbitrary. Why decide on a week? Why not a month? He needs to know if he backtalks today, there will be a consequence today. If he talks back again tomorrow, there will be another consequence tomorrow, and so on. By not extending consequences beyond the day on which the backtalk actually happens, you are showing faith that perhaps tomorrow will be different.

What, you ask nervously, about really important, long-planned events such as band concerts and karate tournaments? The more important the event, the more effective the consequence.

But what if Chucky is to play a solo during the concert and the entire bass section of the band will be hurt if Chucky's consequence for backtalking is to miss the concert. Look at it this way. Chucky made the decision to backtalk, so Chucky's the one—not you—who must figure out how to deal with the bass section. Your parenting job of training is more important than band. If Chucky were ill, he would miss the concert.

But what if Chucky chooses to backtalk ten minutes before you must leave for the band concert and you have an entire squad of dressed-to-the-hilt relatives waiting to go with you? In this case, Chucky's consequence should be to stay home with someone while you take the relatives out to a nice dinner. If there is no one else to stay with Chucky, then do so yourself (parenting often means this kind of sacrifice) and send the others out for a good time. We suggest you have a list of reliable sitters who will come over at a moment's notice.

Disregard any suggestions that Chucky's behavior is your fault, that you are being too extreme, or that you have some nerve, ruining everyone else's good time. Disengage from Chucky's struggle to get you to change your mind.

Say to him, "Chucky, that kind of talk is never acceptable. It uses up my energy. So I won't be taking you to the concert. You will be staying home." To the relatives, you can say, "As a consequence of his backtalk, Chucky will not be going to the concert. He'll be staying with Mrs. Harper. She lives right across the street and can be here in five minutes." The point to remember here is that you'll only have to do this sort of thing once. Chucky won't try it again because now he'll know you mean what you say and that you really are consistent.

And never, ever forget this: after the consequence has been announced, *you must not change your mind about implementing it,* no matter how sweet and loving your child becomes!

When you evaluate your implementation of the consequence in the last part of the four-step section, be ruthless. If the consequence was not logical enough or swift enough, say so.

HOW TO KEEP THE RESOURCES SECTION

At the playground or at parents' group meetings, whenever you meet people who support your backtalk program, record their names and phone numbers in the Resource Section of your workbook. Also record the names of groups that will support your program. As you read some of the books listed in Chapter 13, create an annotated bibliography of helpful sources, being sure to record especially relevant page numbers.

List anything or anyone else who might be helpful. You might even include television shows, films, or compact disc programs that demonstrate effective methods of handling backtalk.

SOME FINAL WORDS ABOUT KEEPING A WORKBOOK

The reason this workbook is called a workbook is because it requires work on your part. The entire backtalk program requires work because it means changing your behavior in response to your child. Change almost always requires work because it is never instant or easy.

As we said earlier, enacting consequences swiftly, the first time, is the hardest work of all. But you can do it if you believe in yourself and in the benefits it will bring to your child.

What if other people you respect, such as teachers, relatives, and adult friends, tell you that your position on backtalk is wrong? Be firm—and read on!

6.

DEALING WITH ADULTS WHO DISAPPROVE OF YOUR STAND ON BACKTALK

Many adults feel that backtalk is permissible. Some consider it normal and even healthy. You need to stand your ground with these people. Some, such as psychiatrists and psychologists, are expendable; you can seek new ones whose views on backtalk are compatible with yours. Others, such as teachers and ex-spouses, are permanent fixtures. In this chapter, you will learn how to deal with these adults without letting them talk you into changing your backtalk policies.

MENTAL HEALTH PROFESSIONALS

A young mother recently called a psychologist on a radio call-in show. The problem, she said, was her ten-year-old son's "mouthiness."

"His what?" the psychologist asked. Apparently she had never heard the term before.

"His mouthiness," the mother repeated. "He says things that are, you know, mouthy."

"Give me an example," the psychologist prompted.

"Well, just last weekend when all our relatives were here, he said I was stupid."

"Why'd he say that?"

"I asked him to do something, and he said right in front of everyone that I was stupid. Then he turned around and told everyone else I was stupid. That's the sort of thing he says all the time. I don't like it."

By saying the boy was mouthy, the mother meant he was a backtalker and she didn't like it. It was a perfect opportunity for the psychologist to address the problem of backtalk.

But instead, she asked the mother what she had done to make the boy think she was stupid. "Why does he call you stupid?" the psychologist asked. "I mean, what sorts of things do you do that might be considered stupid? Let's talk about this. Where is that impression coming from, that you're stupid?"

The mother said she didn't know, that she did not think she was stupid, and that the boy said such things because he was "mouthy."

"Well, now, wait a minute," said the psychologist. "Let's talk about this behavior of yours he thinks is stupid. Who knows, maybe it's something you'd want to think about changing."

There are two problems with this response.

First, this psychologist was dealing not with the form of the boy's communication but with its content. She was seizing and trying to analyze only one of many insults the child undoubtedly hurled at his mother every day. To attempt this kind of analysis with every one of the child's backtalking insults would take forever and would never stop, because the boy probably comes up with new ones all the time.

Second, the psychologist was implying that the mother's behavior had somehow caused her son to perceive her as stupid and that perhaps *she* should modify *her* behavior.

This attitude will not teach the boy to treat others respectfully. It will teach him that it is up to others to watch *their* behavior around *him*. Mother will learn to worry about acting "stupid" again.

But this psychologist's attitude on backtalk—which amounts to an unwillingness to acknowledge that it even exists, let alone that it is disrespectful behavior—is not helpful.

Some books on child-rearing also suggest that backtalk is a form of self-expression which is common among children in our culture. The authors of these books believe this type of self-expression in a symptom of underlying psychological problems that should be diagnosed and treated by mental health professionals.

As the following case history demonstrates, children learn quickly how to use therapy as an excuse to behave disrespectfully.

Case History #7: Jean was babysitting for an agency at night while working at her entry-level publishing job in New York City. Two of her charges, seven-year-old twin boys, were fine the first few times she babysat them, and they told their parents they wanted her back. One night, however, they unleashed a barrage of invective at Jean that was clearly backtalk. When Jean told them she would not tolerate such talk, they replied that their therapist said it was good for them to let adults know how they felt. "Not this adult," said Jean, pointing to herself. That remark started a screamfest which ended only when the boys dropped, exhausted, into their beds and fell asleep.

Later that week the head of the agency called Jean to say that the boys' psychiatrist had told the parents that Jean had set the boys back a year in their treatment and should never be allowed around the children again.

This incident provides a good example of how professional child-rearing experts can encourage parents to idealize and indulge children.

Therapy needs to advocate respect for others and set down guidelines for helping children show respect in their behavior and words.

Your job as a parent is to set limits, provide structure, and teach your children to belong in positive ways. One of the limits they need to learn is that backtalk is not acceptable.

If you take your child to a counselor for backtalk problems, ask yourself the following questions:

- Are you allowed to define the backtalk? Or does the therapist do it for you?
- If you say you don't like the way your child is talking to you, does the therapist validate your feelings, or does he try to make you feel guilty for not liking your child's behavior?
- Are you able to implement the therapist's advice on your own, or do you wish he would move into your home on a full-time basis?
- Is the therapist respectful, firm, and kind to your child?

Answers to these questions will tell you how well the therapist understands and supports your need for a backtalk-free home. If he or she does not support your position, you might want to consider other therapists who believe in respect among family members rather than catering to one member only.

TEACHERS AND OTHER SCHOOL PERSONNEL

There are many wonderful teachers whose very personalities discourage backtalk and elicit respectful behavior from students. The minute children walk into these teachers' classrooms, they know how they are supposed to act and, interestingly, want to act that way because they want these teachers' good opinion.

But other teachers may not support your policy on backtalk. Such teachers tend to fall into the following categories.

The Good Buddy Type. These teachers seem to enjoy backtalk from children. They tend to think backtalk is funny (which it often is, in a biting way), courageous, and a sign of a healthy willingness to question the subject matter being taught.

The Teeth-Grinder. This teacher dislikes backtalk and deals with it by ignoring or avoiding those students who practice it.

The Enabler. These teachers cater to backtalkers (often at the expense of other students) whether they like the backtalk or not, priding themselves on being able to treat backtalk as if it were perfectly normal discourse.

The Captive Audience. This teacher is, to put it bluntly, scared of the backtalker's power and so lets him take over classes by such manipulative means as making fun of the teacher's comments and, on really bad days, hurling ugly insults at the teacher. Good days in this teacher's class are those on which the backtalker is absent. By the middle of the school year, however, other children have learned the art of backtalking so well they can take over when the original problem-makers are not present.

All four of these types of response help teachers deal with

backtalk on a temporary basis. To be fair, it must be said that there is really not much more they can do. More effective methods can result in parental complaints (yes, many parents complain if a child claims he is spoken to firmly in school for any reason) or even lawsuits and possible loss of their jobs. But the teacher responses listed above send the child two important messages: that his backtalk may get him extra attention or even admiration; and that his behavior carries no consequences.

There are also teachers who regard backtalk from students as a sign of neglect at home. When Dr. Ricker's three-year-old son was creating problems in school with his aggressive, dominating behavior, the teacher said there were things she could do at home to help him, such as give him more quality time, encourage him to express his feelings, and never raise her voice to him. There was no way she could know that Dr. Ricker had already built her life around this child. She stayed home with him twenty-four hours a day, took him for all kinds of lessons and enrichment activities, and suffered great frustration as a result of allowing him to express his feelings.

There is, however, another reason why teachers tolerate backtalk: the effect of the progressive movement on schools. It is not that the progressive movement was in favor of disrespect in the classroom, but that it was interpreted by some followers to mean that schools must give children the freedom to do and say whatever they wanted. Formerly models of discipline and authoritarian structure, schools in the 1920s began to reflect these alternative education philosophies. Several, such as the process approach, allowed the child to learn what he wanted to learn when he wanted to learn it, seldom requiring him to learn anything else. Teachers were encouraged to praise every single utterance and effort the child made, even those that were disruptive or mistaken. Any effort to spell, for instance, was loudly applauded as "creative" no matter how incorrect the spelling.

Today most teachers are told that *if they are good teachers,* the children will, in these permissive conditions, learn the subject matter and be cooperative. If the teacher cannot get the child to learn and be cooperative, she has two choices: she can blame herself—as everyone else, from the principal to the child's parents, will encourage her to do—or she can perhaps try to get the child officially diagnosed with a learning disability or an emotional problem.

If your child's teacher allows backtalk in class, you can let her know how you're dealing with your child's backtalk at home. You can tell your child that you can't control what teachers do in their classrooms but you expect good behavior, both at home and at school and there will be consequences for disrespectful behavior at home.

RELATIVES

Extended families that share common beliefs about child rearing are wonderful. Children can go from an aunt's house to a cousin's to a grandparent's house and be welcomed everywhere because they know how to behave in every household.

Some relatives, however, may be fun for your child but hard on you.

The child-rearing experts. These relatives claim to know, just by instinct, how to raise everyone else's children. Any policy that differs from theirs will be met with putdowns and sabotage.

Relatives who think that males can do no wrong. These relatives believe that parents, especially mothers, have no right whatsoever to curb any behavior of the coveted male child.

The next case history demonstrates a grandmother's male-child focus.

Case History #8: The mother of Zina and Rob had brought her children up unequally. "As a girl, I was always supposed to stifle my discontent and do for others," Zina said, "while Rob's discontent was a thing to be feared and placated." She added that "Rob was three years younger than I, and all I heard from my mother the whole time I was growing up was 'Zina, stop whining. You ruin everything for everybody.' But when Rob cried, Mother would say, 'Oh, little Rob is fussing. I have to go see what he wants.'" Her mother's tone would indicate that it was somehow Zina's fault that Rob was unhappy.

Zina's first baby was a boy. "He was dominating and backtalking from an early age. My mother said he was perfect and I should treat him as she had treated Rob." But Zina's husband soon made her realize that if she listened to her mother, her son would turn out like Rob, who was by then a troubled adult who could not hold down a job.

Zina agreed with her husband and overrode her mother's child-rearing advice. Her son was taught to be respectful. Zina's son now is married with a baby daughter. "Guess what?" Zina says. "The first time my son and his wife visited Mother and Dad with the baby, Mother had a fit because she thought the baby was unbearably fussy and annoying. Yet this baby girl was only three weeks old!"

This case history shows that relatives, however well-meaning, may have a separate agenda for your children. In Zina's mother's case, the agenda was that boys are to be worshipped, never allowed to suffer, and never held accountable for anything they say. Girls, however, are to be brought up to serve and to feel guilty about not serving well enough most of the time.

To be fair, however, we must point out that some relatives reverse this gender bias and indulge girl children at the expense of boys.

The in-laws. Some in-laws believe that your child is really theirs, because the child has characteristics of people in their family. Your role is that of nursemaid and, later, governess. Of course, as hired help, you have no right even to identify backtalk, let alone to deal with it. "Never, never stop her from screaming when she doesn't get her way," Karen's mother-in-law tells Karen when her four-year-old daughter has a shrieking temper tantrum. "She's just expressing her personality, which is much more like mine than yours. So I know better what she really needs!"

Doting grandparents. The age group that watches the most network television—about forty hours a week—consists of men and women fifty-five and over. As we'll see in Chapter 10, network situation comedies abound with backtalking children. As one sixty-three-year-old woman explained with a kindly chuckle when I asked her why she watched fourteen (yes, fourteen!) situation comedies religiously, "The families on those shows are so nice, and those kids are so cute, just like my own little grandkids."

Never mind that you, as a child, may have been prevented from backtalking. Now that your parents are grandparents, they see their grandchildren as perfect, and they regard the backtalk as pert, spunky, and adorable—as long as it isn't directed at them. This means your child thinks he can get away with talking back to his parents when he's in the presence of his protective grandma and grandpa.

Wilma, a twenty-six-year-old mother, faces this problem every time she leaves her two-and-a-half-year-old son, Jerry, at her parents' house for an afternoon. When she goes to pick him up, he screams at her to "Go away!" and calls her names. "Oh, now, little Jerry didn't mean anything wrong," Wilma's mother coos when Wilma tells Jerry that kind of speech is unacceptable. "He just hasn't had his nap yet"—or his lunch, or his after-school treat, or his playtime in the park, and he's just sad about having to go home. Jerry never calls his mother a "stinky poo" at home because he knows he'll get an unwanted consequence. But at Grandma and Grandpa's house, he is excused for just about everything.

Wilma should implement the Four-Step Program without delay. She should ignore her parents' attempts to interfere, tell Jerry directly that his backtalk is unacceptable and that, because of it, she is taking him home immediately, even though she had planned to stay awhile and visit. She should not stop for anything enjoyable on the way home. If she does this consistently, the grandparents will soon help reinforce the no-backtalk rule because they'll see that their daughter is serious about it and because they don't want their visits with Jerry to be cut short.

Here are two ways to cope with relatives' interference with your backtalk program:

1. Tell your child that relatives all have their own ideas about what's right, but yours are the only rules that count.
2. Keep your family's rules separate from your relatives' rules. Zina and her husband found this rule crucial in raising their son to be a self-sufficient adult.

FRIENDS

Friends who most heartily disapprove of your stand on backtalk will probably be those whose children either never talked back and those whose children talk back most of the time. Your friends could be like Tricia in the next case history, childless people who, knowing everything there is to know about child-raising, see backtalk as a kind of free speech that must be condoned no matter what.

Case History #9: Hannah, a mother of six-year-old twin girls, had implemented the Four-Step Program for backtalk. Formerly a site of almost constant backtalk and temper tantrums, her home was now a peaceful, happy place. Hannah's husband, Jacques, was delighted with this new atmosphere. The twins were now contented, productive children who were doing well in school and in their music lessons.

Then Hannah's friend from college, Tricia, came to visit. Tricia had majored in early child development, had never married or had children, and was now on sabbatical from the faculty of a large university's education department. Hannah was sure Tricia would be pleased at how well the twins were developing.

On the first day of Tricia's visit, she played with the twins almost nonstop, having a wonderful time. "I feel like a six-year-old myself!" she told Hannah at the end of the day. But on the second day of Tricia's visit, the twins tried backtalking. When Hannah told them it was time to set the table, one twin said, "You can't make me," and the other chimed in, "Me either." This was how they had spoken to their mother all the time in the old days. But now Hannah did not hesitate to deal with the backtalk. She enacted her consequence immediately. "That kind of speech is unacceptable," she said calmly. "As a result of it, you will not be able to eat dinner with us or go to Fun City with us afterward. Mrs. Harper will baby-sit."

"Hannah," cried Tricia, hugging the twins to her, "lighten

up! They didn't say anything wrong." Hannah, however, knew what she had to do to prevent all of her work of the past year from being undone. She took the twins to their room. Upon returning to the kitchen, she began preparing their supper trays and trying to ignore Tricia's look of stunned disapproval. "That's how I handle backtalk now," she told Tricia matter-of-factly.

But Tricia was appalled. "Come on, Hannah!" she cried. "Don't be such a dictator. They were just kidding around with you!"

Hannah was irritated. The Four-Step Program had made a big difference in her life. It was a concept she very much wanted this dear friend to understand, but she decided not to try to defend herself. "I understand why you feel as you do, Tricia, but that's how we handle backtalk in our house," she said firmly. Then she called Mrs. Harper.

Tricia tried several more times during her visit to undermine Hannah's use of the Four-Step Program. Knowing that their new friend Tricia would always take their side, the twins reverted to many former backtalking habits. Hannah, however, never wavered in her use of the four steps and was relieved when Tricia's visit ended. She had learned that friends might mean well when it came to child-raising ideas, but they could not be allowed to interfere with methods that worked.

A month after Tricia left, Hannah was rewarded for her perseverance. She got an E-mail from Tricia saying that, during a two-week visit with another friend who had three children, Tricia had found the children in that home "so incredibly rude" that the "whole house seemed out of control. Because I tried to be friends with these kids, the parents dumped them on me for three whole days while they went off for a weekend alone! I couldn't believe it! What a nightmare! The kids were so awful to me the whole time, so smart-mouthed. Nobody respected me, not the kids or the parents. I had such a nice visit at your home in comparison. Please forgive me for giving you a hard time."

As Hannah's case demonstrates, you should not argue with friends who disapprove of your backtalk program. Avoid using your energy trying to convince them that you have a right to handle your own children. You should either avoid such friends or see them alone, without your children in tow.

If friends are likely to witness you enacting consequences of backtalk upon your children, you should tell them ahead of time what might happen and why. Assure them that even though a consequence—such as taking the backtalker to her room and ignoring her protests—may interrupt a conversation, it should not be a signal for the friend to leave. Social interaction will be resumed again shortly.

As for friends with children who think you are too anal-retentive, obsessive, or incompetent, just remember that they do not have to live with, raise, or be responsible for the character of *your* children. Resist the impulse to say, "Just wait. Someday when you least expect it, your darlings will talk back to you, too." You may need to stay away from such judgmental friends until you feel more competent with your backtalk program. In any case, never let them undermine the norms of communication you want in your household.

EX-SPOUSES

You can always try telling your ex-spouse what you are doing in reaction to backtalk. The ex-spouse may be cooperative or more lenient or more demanding. In either case, you need to explain to your children that they can learn to adapt to two different sets of rules—yours and the other parent's.

Point out to your ex-spouse that in order to be a good single parent, you need to keep your life relatively free of backtalk. You have no time for lack of respect, disruptive behavior, and other displays from your children that sap your energy. Your ex may not need to implement your program at home, but hopefully will encourage the children to respect it in yours.

CAREGIVERS

Find out why your caregiver disapproves of your position on backtalk. It is possible that she adores your child and can't bear to see her constrained in any way. Or perhaps she cares for other children also and can't be worrying just about yours.

The best solution to this problem is to find a new caregiver. But if that solution is not an option, explain the Four-

Step Program to the sitter. Encourage her to be your collaborator. Tell her she will enjoy your child much more if she supports the Four-Step Program as wholeheartedly as possible.

Try having a talk with her every other day or so in which you tell her how your program is going at home and ask if she sees any difference in your child's backtalk. Maybe your conversation will go something like this:

You: Hi, Mary. I'd like to know if Jimmy tried backtalk with you today.

Mary: A little, when the other boys gave me a hard time. He wants to be like them.

You: What did you do?

Mary: With the others, I had to let them be. With Jimmy, I put him in the time-out room right away.

You: How long did he stay?

Mary: Half an hour.

You: How was he when he came out?

Mary: Much better. I wish I could do that with all the kids, but they're too far gone.

You: Great job! You're really good at this! It took me much longer to be able to enact the consequence so well.

Or your exchange could go something like this:

You: What did you do when Jimmy backtalked?

Mary: There was nothing I could do. He's like a dog in a pack with those other boys.

You: Maybe next time you could try a consequence just for Jimmy. Put him in the time-out room.

Mary: He'd say he wasn't being any worse than the other boys.

You: Well, you could tell him you know what his mother would do and so you'll do it, too. He'll understand. I'd appreciate it.

Mary: I could try.

You: I know it's hard. But you could find out how it works.

Mary: I'll try to remember.

You: Great. Just give it a try. Even if it doesn't work, you'll find it interesting.

Meanwhile, keep looking for a caregiver who is willing to respect your wishes and implement the program with your children.

As you've probably realized by now, dealing with all these disapproving people will require confidence. Retain your confidence in your own judgment and you'll be fine. Other people have no idea what's really happening in your home. Only you are there enough of the time to make changes. Only you know how you feel about the way your kids talk to you.

7.

SINGLE PARENTS AND BACKTALK

Single parents often have more problems with backtalk from children than do parents with partners.

Here's why:

1. Children in single-parent families are often brought up to be their parent's friends, having equal say in the relationship. This privilege is more than the children can or need to handle. They try acting grown-up enough to be their parent's buddy, but their version of witty adult-style repartee is actually backtalk.

2. Children in single-parent families are often resentful of lots of things, such as
   - Not having two parents
   - Not seeing their custodial parent or the other parent as often as they'd like
   - Having to act like the father or mother of the household when they'd rather be goofing off

- Never having enough money
- Never getting enough attention

This is not to say such challenges are bad (these children often develop an admirable sense of responsibility), but these deficiencies can make children feel resentful, and this resentment may be expressed in backtalk.

3. Friends of children in single-parent families are often children of single parents, also. These peer groups tend to validate and even encourage one another's use of backtalk.

4. Backtalk by children of single parents is usually effective. The single parent often feels so tired, lonely, worried, and guilty that she sees the child's backtalk as somehow her fault and gives in to whatever it is intended to accomplish.

5. Single parents have no one at home to consult on their children's behavior. Thus the parent may not even realize that backtalk is anything other than normal communication, because there is no one close to tell her so.

6. The single parent's unmitigated admiration of the child can become so unrealistic that she thinks backtalk is as wonderful as everything else the child says. Feelings of pain caused by the backtalk are numbed by her intense love for the child.

But none of these reasons makes the backtalk acceptable.

In fact, children of single parents are especially in need of knowing backtalk is not permissible. They have to make a life with less help than other children get, and so need a particularly clear realization that backtalk will impede, not increase, their chances for happiness and success.

THE SINGLE PARENT AND THE FOUR-STEP PROGRAM

The single parent, despite her problems, may be more fortunate than parents with partners in at least one respect—there is nobody at home to subvert her implementation of a backtalk-prevention plan.

First, the single parent must decide what the consequences of backtalk can be. Not watching television? Not going to Burger King on weekends? Not going to the dollar movies on Friday nights? Not having company over to spend the night? All these could be consequences if they are logically connected to the backtalk in words delivered matter-of-factly and without spite. For instance, a mother could say, "That kind of tone and those kinds of words are not acceptable in this household. The way you're speaking to me uses up my time and energy so I'm not using my time and energy to take you to Burger King for dinner."

Second, the single parent must realize her children are not her friends. They are children in need of a parent.

Third, the single parent must find out what he can do to

improve life with the child. Should he spend more time with the child and less with his adult friends? Or should he spend less time with the child and get a life of his own? Annie, a single mother of twin daughters, was so completely devoted to their junior chorus activities that she had no life of her own whatsoever. All her pleasure came from watching her girls, dressed in costumes she had made them, singing solos or duets at concerts. Every time she tried to discourage their ever-escalating backtalk, they would threaten to quit chorus—a consequence Annie could not bear to contemplate. When the girls dropped out of chorus in high school to pursue other activities, Annie went through months of withdrawal and had to use therapy to become her own person. Had she implemented the backtalk program when the girls were younger, she might have been able to disengage from the girls' lives enough to find a life for herself years earlier.

There are other issues to be considered by the single parent. Is the child too often left with relatives or sitters? And, especially important in single-parent families in which the single parent is often tired, worried, and deprived of many adult pleasures, is the parent attentive and respectful when he is with the child?

All these areas can be improved, no matter how little time and money there is. The backtalk-prevention program can be instituted at the same time. The next case history shows the type of groundwork the single parent needs to lay so he can make the Four-Step Program work.

Case History #10: Sam, a forty-year-old single father,

dealt with the escalating backtalk of his three sons by going out every night after work, and enjoying ski and scuba trips by himself every weekend, leaving the boys with his mother. When he tried thinking of a logical consequence to enact, none came to mind that the boys might care about. He never took them anywhere so he could not remove that pleasure. He supposed he could try not buying them things they wanted, such as sports equipment, but he used such purchases to ease the guilt he felt at being away from them so much. He realized that his whole life was so disengaged from theirs that his implementation of the Four-Step Program was almost impossible.

Unwilling to give up his weekend trips, he arranged to take all three boys with him. At first, the effort and expense were daunting, but the boys soon became adept at cooperating and helping organize the trips. They also learned to eat food brought from home and to share rented skis and snorkel equipment. At the same time they learned not to backtalk because there were now so many activities they didn't want to miss—the scuba diving, the skiing, the socializing with the children they met on these trips.

Sam resumed his parenting role and became less selfish and more respectful. This attitude, along with his provision of many pleasures for the boys, made the backtalk program very effective in Sam's home.

SPECIAL DAY CARE PROBLEMS FOR
SINGLE PARENTS

Many caregivers take a rather superior attitude toward single parents. They feel that day care provides a better environment than the single-parent home. The child and mother may buy into this attitude and, subconsciously, expect less of the child's behavior at home and believe backtalk is to be expected.

Stop! You're the parent. You're the one the child needs the most no matter what you provide. You're the one who can deal with your child's backtalk. You can be glad your sitter provides your child with so much pleasure, but you don't have to feel insecure in comparison.

Some caregivers, however, think you're so desperate you can't possibly replace them. They give your child minimal care but not much else. So of course you figure your neglected, frustrated child has a right to backtalk at night.

No, he does not have that right, even under bad circumstances. To allow him to backtalk is to teach him that backtalk is a way of coping with bad breaks in life.

Start looking for a better caregiver.

8.

WORKING PARENTS AND BACKTALK

Despite talk of an ever-stronger economy, the reality is that, in most families, both parents have to work. Many working parents are exhausted and preoccupied with holding on to the jobs they have that support their families. As a result, it's not uncommon for working parents — both single and married — to feel anger.

We're not talking about a parent's anger at his children, but his anger at the job, his boss, his co-workers, and his spouse or partner who does not seem to be pulling her weight. If this anger never gets resolved, if a job situation is unsatisfactory, the parent or parents may come home seething every night. The children pick up on this anger. They act out their own anger at school, at friends, and at the parents for being so tired and angry during the few hours they see them. Part of this acting out is backtalk.

A sad cycle is begun. In some families the parents may yell at the children, the children talk back to the parents, the parents reply rudely, and the house becomes a hotbed of harsh words. In other homes the children backtalk, the parents refuse to say anything, and the house becomes an icebox of cold dislike of everyone in it. Dinner, if the family eats together, is silent and brief. Everyone retires to his or her room as soon as possible.

Weekends can start out better, when everyone is refreshed after a good night's sleep, but the mood often deteriorates rapidly when a child starts backtalking at the first provocation—or sometimes without a provocation. This backtalk negatively affects the good mood of the family. By sundown, hostility prevails.

These dreadful scenarios can easily become the at-home lifestyle of working parents, no matter how well-meaning they may be. However, things can be changed. By using the Four-Step Program, working parents can eliminate the backtalk and improve the quality of family members' time together.

First, the parents must decide on the mood of family life and the type of communication they will allow in their home. Second, the working parents must choose consequences that they have the time and energy to enact in the event of backtalk. Here is a simple scenario that can be used as a guide. We'll call the daughter Ceci and say she's about thirteen.

Mother (just home from work and very tired): Ceci, it's your turn to cook tonight. Thank goodness! (She sinks down in her favorite chair). I had a terrible day.
Ceci (in her cheerleader uniform, drops her pom-pom):

Duh? I'm supposed to cook tonight? I don't think so. *Mother (wanting to lash back because she feels hurt and angry that Ceci has no empathy for her fatigue, but remembering to start the backtalk-prevention program instead):* Ceci, that kind of response is not acceptable or respectful. As a result of it, I will not use the little bit of time and energy I have left to take you to the game. *Ceci:* But I'm on the cheerleading squad! *Mother:* I'll be upstairs taking a bubble bath if you need me. I'll fix my own dinner later. (She leaves the room.)

If Ceci apologizes for her tone and fixes a proper dinner, should Mother relent? No, and she should avoid all further discussion. The idea is to show, not just to tell, Ceci that her backtalk has consequences that are real and cannot be negotiated away.

Because of fatigue and feelings of frustration from their jobs, working parents will need willpower to make the Four-Step Program work. Where, in view of the physical and mental overload suffered by most working parents, will this determination come from? The mother in the following case history provides one workable answer.

Case History #11: Myra is a working mother of three children, age eight, fourteen, and seventeen. She not only works full time as a secretary in a government office but has been taking three college courses a semester for the past six years. She was expecting to graduate with a B.S. in business administration at the time she was interviewed for this book. Her husband is the editor of a regional newspaper who is also responsible for running the presses. He is required to work at least sixty hours a week, just to keep his job.

And yet a neighbor, who spends much time with this family, says they have the happiest family life imaginable. How do the parents manage this? "I know it sounds simple, but we are just too busy to be unhappy," Myra said. "There's no time for bad feelings in our house."

The children are always busy with assigned household chores and other responsibilities. The seventeen-year-old son, for instance, is responsible for helping the eight-year-old improve his reading skills. The fourteen-year-old daughter is responsible for the family laundry—a constant, daunting job. The mother is responsible for driving the daughter to her soccer practice and games—no easy task, since the daughter's team has been in championship playoffs for the past five years—and the older son to his academic decathlon meets. The father is responsible for driving the younger son to soccer practice and coaching the soccer team. All family members have assigned jobs even when they're on much-looked-forward-to family camping trips in their recreational vehicle.

But Myra admits that there's another explanation for the family's happiness besides lack of time for unhappiness. "We're always glad to see each other at the end of the day," she says. "I'm always glad to see them, anyway, and maybe that feeling is contagious." When asked if she didn't get too tired to be glad to see anybody with her hectic schedule, she said, "Yes, I get tired and frustrated and I wish I had a better job or better teachers—some of my courses are such a drag. But then I make myself remember how crazy I am about my family. I need them. I love having them around. I love cooking for them, and I insist we always, except on very rare occasions, eat dinner together. Some people like having no family—not me."

Asked what she did when the children got argumentative or difficult, she said, "We don't drive them where they want to go, such as to a friend's house or to the mall to meet friends. In the case of our older son, we don't let him use the car."

This case history demonstrates some principles of the Four-Step Program in action. One is that backtalk is not an option in this household. Another is that the parents provide so much for the children—so much attention, so many services, such as driving, and so much support for the children's activities—that potential consequences abound.

This case history also demonstrates the need for *self-discipline*. The parent must act as though she's happy to come home to the family no matter how she is feeling. Many experts insist that acting as if you are happy soon makes you actually feel happy.

To reiterate—creating and sustaining a happy family life is necessary for steps 2, 3, and 4. Without a happy family life, few consequences can have much impact, no matter how immediately they are enacted.

The working parent has another potential backtalk-causing

situation besides lack of time, energy, and job security: having to leave children alone after school. These "latchkey" children need to be dealt with by telephone if you can't be there in person.

Bob, an advertising executive whose wife, a drug sales representative, worked out of town most of the time, was faced with caring alone for their twelve-year-old son, Sean. Sean had told his father that having an after-school babysitter was for wimps and he wanted to stay by himself. Every afternoon when Bob called from work to check on Sean, their exchange went along these lines:

Bob: Hi, guy!
Sean: Dad, please — do you have to call every day?
Bob: Just checking, kid. It makes me feel better to know . . .
Sean: Well, get over it!
Bob: Hey, I worry about you!
Sean: Well, deal with it! I gotta go. Moe's here, we're watching MTV.
Bob: MTV? I thought I told you —
Sean: Bye, Dad (click and dial tone).
Bob (sheepishly to co-worker who overhears Bob's end of the conversation every day): Kids these days! What're you gonna do?

Here is the way the conversation should have gone:

Bob: Hi, guy! How was school?

110

Sean: Okay, but I got a C-minus on my math test.

Bob: Math is tough. Let's find a tutor.

Sean: I hate doing that. I'll feel like a baby.

Bob: I understand how you feel, but I bet you'll be more comfortable in math class if you get some help. How about this? We find a tutor and you agree to give her an honest chance for, oh, say, a month.

Sean: I guess that's fair. Where do we find a tutor?

Bob: Your math teacher might know a high school student who's qualified. We'll ask him first. If not, I'll call the math department at the university.

Sean: Okay. How's your day going?

Bob: Not bad, we got that new account. Well, I'd better go. Have fun at soccer practice.

Sean: See you tonight. Bye.

If the Sean in this conversation sounds too good to be true, rest assured he is not. Because he knows backtalk is not acceptable, he uses these checking-in conversations for exchanging information, seeking support, solving problems, and other positive purposes that make him and his father feel better, even when the news is not glowing, as in the case of the math grade.

What Bob and other working parents with latchkey children must do is take charge. Finding a sitter or some kind of cooperative child-care arrangement or supervised after-school activity is essential, no matter what the children say. Also essential is applying the Four-Step Program at home and

on the telephone. Parents can't threaten or enact consequences from work, but they can do so at home. "The way you
speak to me over the phone is not acceptable," the parent can
announce immediately after reaching home. "I'm not allowing
you to have company after school anymore, because I don't
want anyone else to hear your tone. The housekeeper will be
here instead." Or even better, "I'll be taking my lunch hour
every day when you get home from school so I can drive you
to the YMCA"—or the tennis club or anywhere else where
you have made arrangements for an adult to watch your child
after school. When he protests, you can disengage by doing
what you have to do—going back to work.

Working parents must have two firm rules: One is that a
good mood in the home is worth working for no matter how
tired and discouraged the parents may feel. The second is that
the backtalk-prevention program can be applied successfully
in the few hours working parents spend with their children—
and it should be, if those hours are to be productive and
happy for all concerned.

9.
DEALING WITH YOUR CHILDREN'S BACKTALKING FRIENDS

Because backtalk has reached epidemic proportions among children in all socioeconomic brackets, it's sure to be demonstrated by many of your children's friends in your home—not by just any friends, either, but often by your child's favorite friends. Children seem to admire their more assertive peers, and the latter are exactly the sort most likely to backtalk. Of course children admire these friends because they're not afraid of anyone, not their parents or anyone else's.

Some parents are horrified to find out their children talk back to adults in other people's homes. But other parents refuse to worry about it. Why not? The main, overarching reason is that there is no longer any stigma associated with other parents' bad opinion of one's child. Unless the other parents have social or financial leverage over the backtalkers' parents, the latter have no real reason to care what they think. A second reason, as demonstrated by the following case history, is that some parents are proud of, if not actually afraid of, these willful children of theirs.

Case History #12: Naomi, the daughter of a fire-and-brimstone preacher, was married to Roy, the son of strict Calvinist parents. Soon after their wedding, they left home, determined to live in a more liberal, permissive culture. They allowed their daughter, Marin, to develop as she pleased, never having to compromise with anyone or any institution. Roy and Naomi looked with tenderness upon her temper tantrums and her dominating put-downs of neighborhood children.

When a neighbor complained to Naomi that Marin, then four, had told her daughter to get out of the sandbox and not come back, Naomi shrugged and said, in a tone tinged with admiration of her daughter, "Well, you just don't say no to Marin." Both Naomi and Roy kept on saying that every time Marin enraged a teacher or a peer's parent, which was just about every week for the rest of the time she spent with her parents.

When Marin was twenty-seven, Naomi and Roy finally had to say no to her: "No, you cannot stay here without a job or college degree with your baby." After tearing up their house in a temper tantrum, Marin did move out. Her parents have heard from her only a few times, once to say she'd given up the baby for adoption, which Naomi figures financed Marin's nonworking lifestyle for another few years. Another time, Marin called to say she was on antidepressants and could she come home for a while. The answer was no again.

"We had learned to live peacefully without her and didn't want things in an uproar again," Naomi said.

Naomi is philosophical about Marin. "I was always afraid of her," she said. "She's so dominating and aggressive, and I'm so mellow; there was no hope." Naomi is very disappointed that Marin's strong personality did not make her rich and famous. "I really thought she'd be the head of a company or a politician by now," Naomi said wonderingly. "She had what it took — I don't know where she went wrong."

The point of this case history is that if Roy and Naomi had taken the parents of Marin's friends seriously, they might have realized there was a problem that they needed to address. They might have stopped putting up with Marin's backtalk, also. And Marin might have learned how to channel her strong personality more productively. But Marin's parents chose to ignore the red flags that other adults had raised, throughout their daughter's childhood.

"I just told them, 'You don't say no to Marin,'" Naomi repeated. "I was getting calls every few days, every time she was invited to someone's house. And for a while, she was invited out a lot because she was very popular." Then, of course, the invitations stopped coming — the friends' parents finally learned to say no to having Marin visit. Still true to their liberal child-rearing beliefs, Naomi and Roy see no connection between Marin's backtalk of friends' parents and her difficulty in adjusting to adult life.

A third reason why parents don't care if their children talk back to other children's parents is simple unwillingness to deal with the child's backtalk. Handling the backtalk is just not on the parents' list of things to do or of concerns to be addressed. Case history #13 demonstrates this situation vividly.

Case History #13: Deirdre and Sidney have an amicable divorce. Both are very successful, high-powered business people in a large southwestern city. Both work hard and play hard, often vacationing alone or with friends in such places as Aspen, the Alps, and the Caribbean. They share custody of their children—Lily, age ten, and Larry, eight—who are, Deirdre admits matter-of-factly, superfluous to their lives. "We never should have had kids," she says now.

She's very realistic about the children's problems. "They have such smart mouths they get thrown out of schools and friends' homes. But Sidney and I have decided not to worry about that problem right now. We have the children in a private school eight months of the year and in summer camps the rest of the time." When the children do come home on vacations, they are cared for by sitters, often around the clock. "Frankly, we tend to put all our energy into our jobs because we're at the prime of our careers," Deirdre explained. "Once we took the children on a cruise to Alaska, but they were such little hellions that we turned them over to the steward for the entire trip." The children, she added, will figure out on their own how to act when they want friends badly enough.

This child-rearing strategy may be satisfactory for Sidney and Deirdre. But it leaves other adults to deal with the children's backtalk. Unfair? Of course. But it is all too common.

The problem is manageable, however, for host parents who find themselves entertaining backtalkers. The following case history shows how it can be done.

Case History #14: Amy, a television producer, was having a sleepover party for Justine, her nine-year-old daughter. The guest of honor was Kelly, a young friend of Justine's who had just gotten a big part in a television sitcom. Amy and her husband had known Kelly's parents for years and knew that once Kelly started working in her show, she would have little time for old friends.

From the time Kelly arrived at the party, she showed a new and disturbing attitude. She was rude to the other guests and to Justine. Finally, when Amy told the girls to stop squirting her husband's shaving cream on one another, Kelly talked back to Amy directly. "You can't make me do anything, Amy," she said, using Amy's first name for the first time. "You're not my mother."

"Yeah, Mom," said Justine, trying to sound brave. But to Kelly, she added with a warning tone in her voice, "Kell, you shouldn't have said that. I told you!" Justine knew exactly what was going to happen.

Amy could have said many things to Kelly, such as "But this is my house" or "But your mother wouldn't want you to act this way" or "I don't care, you have to watch your attitude with me." But instead, she enacted a logical consequence.

"Kelly," she said, "you'll have to leave. That kind of talk is not acceptable in our house. Please get dressed immediately." Ignoring the loud protests from the other guests, Amy called

Kelly's mother, stood over Kelly until she was dressed and ready to go, and showed her the door when Kelly's mother arrived. "I'll be happy to entertain Kelly again," Amy told Kelly's mother with a confident smile, "but I'll have to do the same thing if she speaks to me disrespectfully."

If you need to know how the other guests reacted to this scene, you need more understanding of step 4, disengaging from the struggle. The truth is, as Amy knew, it doesn't matter how the guests reacted. "Who cares what they thought?" Amy said. "I told them there would be no more use of the shaving cream that night. I disregarded the looks of fury and shock on the guests' faces, said I hoped they'd have a good time from then on, and went into the bedroom to read." Justine later told Amy the rest of the party went well enough, but that Kelly's departure put a real damper on the guests' mood. "I'm not surprised," Amy replied. "It's too bad that Kelly behaved the way she did." She did not apologize, emphasize, or in any other way discuss her use of consequence at the party and went on to discuss another subject entirely. The case of the backtalking party guest was closed forever.

This is the best, most logical consequence for guests who backtalk: ejecting them immediately and calmly from your home. If their parents are off on a month-long safari and can't be reached, these backtalkers can be treated with the same consequences you'd use on your own children.

And remember—immediate ejection of the backtalker as

a consequence for backtalking is not only impressive to the backtalker but serves as a dramatic show of strength to your children as well. The message sent is that you care enough about the tone of communication in your home to act on it immediately.

10.

DEALING WITH BACKTALK ON TELEVISION AND IN THE OTHER MEDIA

Research indicates that the mainstream media have a direct effect on children's behavior. Most of the studies show that children usually want to emulate the types of behavior in the media that arouse their emotions, whether pleasurable or painful. This arousal is visceral and involuntary.

One study showed that the sight of karate fighting on television made children want to kick other children on the playground. Another study showed that aggressive behavior increased sharply after children watched films containing any kind of violence. Thus it stands to reason that if children see backtalk in their favorite movies and TV shows, they will have an increased urge to indulge in backtalk.

Children see backtalk on the big and small screens all the time. Television shows and films featuring child characters almost always contain backtalk. One evening of scorekeeping showed that all prime-time shows featuring children had at least two incidents of backtalk per episode, usually more.

By backtalk in such mainstream media as film and television, we mean backtalk during the course of normal conversations between and among characters, usually in the form of put-down one-liners meant to evoke laughter. The younger the character doing the backtalk, the more charming it is supposed to be. These backtalking children are represented not as brats but as normal, well-behaved children who are in most other ways obedient to their parents.

In the mainstream media, backtalk is presented not as unacceptable behavior to be met with logical consequences but as a winning strategy that results in instant submission and even admiration from its adult targets. Most backtalk on television is heard on talk shows and sitcoms; most backtalk in films is seen in the popular genre featuring teenage miscreants and their younger siblings, who imitate the rude teenagers.

In these and other films like them, the backtalkers are represented as attractive, desirable, smart, and often funny. Their self-confidence, standing among peers, and entertainment quotient are shown in their backtalk to peers, teachers, parents, and other adults in authoritative positions.

The backtalk targets almost always deserve the backtalk they get for any number of reasons, such as stuffed-shirt behavior, too-earnest behavior, disciplinary behavior (justified or not), or self-righteous behavior (in which the backtalked character insists on chastity or temperance or some other "old-fashioned" virtue). Often, many different justifications of backtalk are shown in the same film or television show. So the child viewer is provided with all kinds of reasons to use backtalk every time he watches TV or goes to the movies.

Here are some other reasons why the mainstream media have so much influence over children when it comes to backtalk:

1. Young people of all ages think that anything shown on television (except news and other shows about actual people) is not only okay, it's desirable.

2. Mainstream television and film characters are made to seem like members of popular social cliques. They look and act in ways that set standards of appearance and behavior for others.

3. Children viewers not only want to be like these characters, they want their friends to know they are the kind of people these characters are. So the viewers want to have the same clothes, hairstyles, and body type as the characters. They must also use the same gestures and speech patterns.

4. The one-liner retort delivered so well by media characters becomes a skill to be practiced. In real-life children, however, the use of such retorts amounts to backtalk.

Since the media are such an important source, teacher, and validator of backtalk among children, they merit some analysis.

A BRIEF HISTORY OF BACKTALK IN POPULAR CULTURE

Until the early 1960s television and film tried to appeal to adults. Adults had to be pleased, not children, because they controlled the purse strings. They decided which advertised products to buy and which films to attend. Backtalking children in films were seen rarely, and most of them were "bad boy" types in Little Rascals, Three Stooges, and other comedy movies. Backtalking children on television were marginalized to roles of semi-delinquent friends of good children. *Leave It to Beaver* had Eddie Haskell and *Happy Days* had the Fonz.

In the late 1960s and early 1970s, two social developments caused children's status to be elevated from that of dependent beings who had to be cared for, who should be seen and not heard, and who should always do as they were told, to that of desirable beings who should be catered to and could behave in any way they chose.

The first development that changed children's status was the breakdown of the nuclear family. It had three results:

1. Children became the interpreters of modern culture.

2. Various forms of popular culture preached that youthfulness was highly desirable.
3. The soaring divorce rate made children of suddenly single parents their parents' new best friends whose approval was to be sought, bought, begged, and in other ways striven for.

The second development that contributed to the change in children's status in society was the growth of children's economic power. Suddenly they had more money of their own to spend, thanks to generous allowances, jobs of their own, and savings from generous cash gifts, and they got to decide how the family's money would be spent. They could now make their parents buy them things—clothes, makeup, hairstyling, and, more recently, cosmetic surgery—to make them more like their ideal images. And their ideal images, of course, were their most adored television characters.

The result of these two developments can be described in a single sentence: Children were now considered smarter, not to mention more amusing and appealing, than adults. Or, to put it even more simply, suddenly to be young was to be powerful.

Catching on quickly, the mainstream media now showed children as adorable savants who were given the last word in most verbal exchanges.

COMMERCIALS AND BACKTALK

Commercials showed the new glamorous status of children more clearly than any other mainstream media form. As one marketing expert put it, commercials were now designed not just to sell products to children but to use children as marketing tools to attract consumers in other age groups. Commercials routinely featured children who were smarter than their unsophisticated parents. In one commercial, a child talks back to his obviously overstressed working mother, speaking blatantly and rolling his eyes, until she buys him the product the commercial is advertising.

Needless to say, such commercials not only give children viewers permission to use backtalk but tell them that backtalk is cool and effective. Despite this empowerment of youth on television, researchers report that teens' and children's television viewing has declined from about forty hours a week in 1980 to approximately twenty hours a week in 1995. But that's probably due to the popularity of video games, computer games, and the Internet. Children age two to five watch the most TV—approximately twenty-five hours a week. (Other experts claim the television-viewing figures for young people are actually much higher.)

WHAT TO DO ABOUT MEDIA BACKTALK

The best way to deflect media-driven backtalk is to start by watching the backtalk-laden shows and movies with your children. Let them know, after the program is over, that the kind of speech shown would not be acceptable in your home. "It might be okay in that television family, I suppose," you can say, "but not in this family." Be very clear about what part of the backtalk you did not like.

For instance, in one popular, PG-rated film about and for children, the main character lets loose a hostile barrage of backtalk at a social worker, which ends with the child calling the man a dick.

"I don't like the tone, the words, or the obscenity that little boy used," you could say.

"But," your child could protest, "the man he said those words to was not a good person. The man deserved to be insulted."

You can reply with one or more of several messages. Here are five suggestions:

1. "Children can tell the truth and still be respectful, without using backtalk." Have your child come up with examples for the child in the film. How could he let the adult know what he thinks of him without being disrespectful? Both you and your child can try out examples.

2. "That child is a character in a film, like a made-up character in a storybook; he isn't a real child. That kind of behavior is not acceptable in our home." You are now performing the important task of separating real life from the media.

3. "Insults and obscenities are not acceptable forms of speech in our home. Period." The child will never again have to wonder if he can get away with insults and obscenities.

4. "You may laugh, but you should never speak to me or anyone else that way in real life." You are telling the child that what may be funny in the film is not going to be amusing in real life.

5. After watching a show such as *Roseanne* on television: "You should never speak to people that way. And I promise you that neither I nor your father nor any other adult in our house will ever speak to you the way Roseanne does her children." This choice acknowledges that backtalk by adults is also unacceptable.

Watching TV and movies with your child involves time and interaction with him—both of which are important. This process also helps the child understand the kind of communication you do and do not want before he tries it out and faces a consequence.

USING THE MEDIA AS A TEACHING TOOL

1. Find a videotape that you know contains examples of backtalk and watch it with the child, remote control in hand so that you can pause at appropriate moments.
2. Watch a film with him you've never seen and point out backtalk when you come to it, or ask your child to identify the backtalk.
3. Videotape the more backtalk-laden television shows and watch them with him, pausing at the teaching moments.
4. Watch a television show with him as it airs. Then turn off the television and discuss the backtalk incidents.
5. Discuss commercials that show backtalking kids.

VIDEO GAMES AND BACKTALK

One mother said her son's backtalk was so escalated by video games that she and her husband had to seek help. Here is her story:

Case History #15: Ron, age ten, was obviously affected by his two favorite video games—both fighting games that involved a great deal of violence and gore. His very favorite was a role-playing game, in which he got to be a robot whose arms, legs, and other anatomical parts were lethal weapons he could use to kill enemy robots. The other was a standard fighting game with cartoonlike characters that could be operated with various strategic moves of the game controls.

Both games made him nervous and keyed up while he was playing them, but he acted hostile for hours after he finished playing the robot game. It also led to backtalk that his parents found very alarming. "Get off my back!" he would say to his mother when she asked him to put away his game cartridges. "I'm busy" was another standard post–video game backtalk reply, and "I don't need this!" was yet another.

Finally his parents realized that Ron saw himself as the menacing, all-powerful, planet-saving robot for several hours after he stopped playing that game. "He would play before school," said his mother, "then have to be dragged away, back-talking wildly, to catch the school bus. The minute he got home in the afternoon, he would return to the game and stay at it till we got home from work and made him come to dinner." The sitter, who was otherwise fine, allowed Ron to play his games because he needed no watching when he did so. "But I doubt she could have gotten him to do anything else anyway," Ron's mother sighed. "He was so devoted to his games he would have put up a fuss the sitter could never have handled."

It was not until Ron's teacher complained about his in-school backtalk that the parents realized they needed to take drastic action. "The teacher said she would have to expel him from school if the backtalk did not stop. It was an excellent school, and we didn't want that to happen."

So Ron's parents started the Four-Step Program. The consequence enacted for Ron's postgame backtalk was immediate loss of the game for the day. The next day he could try again to see if he could control his backtalk. After losing game privileges every day for a week, Ron stopped backtalking.

Ron's parents also got him into a basketball program. "We found an after-school camp that was oriented toward basketball, and we put up a hoop in our backyard." Ron is now on a youth league team, and he's usually too busy, physically spent, and happy—his game is improving all the time—to worry about video games. "He now regards games as something little kids play but that he's outgrown," his mother said, "but he'd be more into the games than ever if we hadn't done something about this problem."

This case shows that video games—many of which feature nonstop combat, hatred, and competition—can lead to the use of backtalk as another kind of weapon.

TALK SHOWS AND BACKTALK

Like video games, talk shows need a separate section in this chapter on media and backtalk. Frequently crisis-ridden and very melodramatic, talk shows often deal with children. And the children they show often demonstrate one real skill—

backtalking their parents, the host, and members of the audience from the beginning of the show to the end.

Children on these shows generally indulge in four kinds of backtalk:

1. *Mocking.* An offstage camera shows the children laughing and jeering as they watch their mother on the dressing room monitor while she is sobbing out her story of the children's uncontrollable behavior. The worse the story becomes, the more the children, still backstage, cheer and mockingly imitate their sobbing mother.

2. *Insolent body language.* Once onstage, the children indulge in much rolling of eyes and shrugging of shoulders and shaking of their heads as the mother begs them to understand what their behavior is doing to the family, the mother, the teachers, or whoever else is involved.

3. *Shaming.* The mother is accused of being stupid— "Oh, you don't know anything" is a common putdown by children of mothers on talk shows—or some other inadequacy.

4. *Getting in the last word.* The backtalk on talk shows ends not when the mother says so but when the child decides. Backtalk statements that end the conversations include "I don't care" and "Send me to live with Daddy." Another conversation stopper is typical of

unwed mothers living at home, many of whom are pregnant again: "You can try to make me stay home with my baby every night, but I'm not going to do it." The backtalker then looks at her nails, sits back, swings her leg, refuses to say another word, and seems to be very satisfied with herself. Why shouldn't she be? She has everyone around under control.

At this point the talk show psychologist may be called upon. This expert's advice to mother and child is usually that they listen to each other's needs and go to counseling. Then, getting stern, this therapist warns that the mother must get the daughter under control or the daughter will wind up a delinquent on the streets and the mother will be in a mental ward, if she's not dead. Such short-term balms and long-term caveats are all these psychologists can do in approximately fifteen minutes. They can barely squeeze in the declaration that both mother and daughter need professional help before the credits start running and the show ends.

These shows demonstrate vividly and dramatically what can happen when parents fail to curb backtalk by enacting consequences. On one show about daughters whose behavior was out of control, Sally Jessy Raphael threatened to put the child off the show if the backtalk continued. But she never did enact that consequence and so the rude language continued.

Trying another tack, Sally Jessy pleaded, "Look how you're treating your mother," as the mother sobbed and had to be handed tissue. The rude teenager shrugged and said her mother's tears were her problem.

Your children, if they watch these shows, must understand that you, as a parent will never let things get anywhere near this far, and that they, as your children, will never be allowed to associate with such a rude child.

In addition to talking to your children about the media, you need to find ways to provide them with a life so busy and productive (Ron's parents did that when they got Ron into basketball) that your children cannot, and really do not want to, relate to the kinds of children they see on television and in the movies.

11.

DEALING WITH BACKTALK FROM CHILDREN IN COLLEGE

Whether children go away to college or commute from home, most college students—especially freshmen—will backtalk their parents in a way that is particularly unbearable. Backtalk from college students makes parents feel old, obsolete, anachronistic, slow-witted, and unable to measure up to the child's new standards for adults he admires. Even if the parent is spending $20,000 a year on the child's education, she will still get what we call college-kid backtalk.

College students tend to backtalk parents, even if they've never done so before, for one or more of the following reasons:

- They are hanging out with new friends.
- They are finding their identities and remaking themselves.
- They are feeling pressures they've never felt before.

- They are firmly convinced that you, the parent, have no idea what they're going through.

In other words, they are becoming new people who are responsible for themselves now and living independently for the first time. As emerging adults who are (almost) your peers, they often test your boundaries by such actions as backtalk.

But of course these students think they have good reasons for treating you disrespectfully. Here are some of those specific reasons. Yes, we know — most sound incredibly superficial, but lots of college students take them very seriously.

Your Academic Worth Is Questioned. You never heard of Spinoza? Or bell hooks? And you've been passing yourself off as knowledgeable all these years?

There is nothing like a good survey course in Western civilization or English literature or art history — and the freshman is probably taking all three — to make the student feel he knows everything and you folks back home know nothing.

"I can't believe," he tells you, "you still think Karl Marx is a bad guy" — or that you refuse to replace your paintings on velvet with cubist prints. "Provincials," he cries in a sincerely disgusted, denouncing tone, or if he hasn't yet learned that word, he may call you ignoramuses or something similar. "Intellectual peasants, that's what you are." You, his parents, who have scrimped and saved and planned financially and done without Caribbean cruises so your child could have this experience, are in a special kind of pain. If he's less outspoken, he may still roll his eyes and say "Duh!" in a way that causes just as much hurt.

Your Ethics Are Hopelessly Obsolete. You have brought your son up to disapprove of cheaters, and now his roommate brags about never writing his own papers. Suddenly you seem old-fashioned and rigid. "You and Dad don't realize that socializing in college, networking, is as important as getting good grades. If that means hiring people to help out, hey, that's just good management."

Your Child Was Not Tapped for Sigma Chi. It just has to be your fault for not getting him the right tutors, not teaching him the right social graces, not buying him the right kind of clothes or car, not knowing the code for membership in the upper class.

Your Child's Studies Interfere with His Social Life. He goes out every night with friends until 2:00 A.M., then sleeps through his morning classes the next day. Actually, he feels guilty, knows you have a right to be mad, and is going to get mad at you first. So he decides you would never understand the realities of college life today.

Take heart. All of these types of behavior are just phases. The student finds out that cheaters often get caught or inevitably face a teacher who makes them write their papers in class, that campus social life is often more trouble than it's worth, and that partying all night will land him on academic probation after just one semester.

However, no excuse should justify the college student's

backtalk. She may be able to cut classes, consort with unconventional friends, and do whatever else she wants at school, but she should not be allowed to backtalk her parents.

HOW TO COPE

Whatever the reason for your child's backtalk, you can institute the Four-Step Program as soon as you are subjected to it.

One logical consequence you can choose if she's living at home is to get her out. Don't tell her to leave; she won't believe you mean it. Just put her belongings in the yard, redo her room as a sewing center, and start using it. The whole process should take less than four hours. They will be four terrible hours, to be sure, but that will be it. You and your college-age child can now get on with your lives.

The next case history tells how one mother enacted this consequence.

Case History #17: Hilary and Jack and their son, Bart, had always been close, sharing a love of trips, board games, and silly movies that enabled them to enjoy one another more with every passing year. When Bart was in high school, his closest friends were always included in the family circle. Because of this happy relationship, Hilary and Jack always assumed Bart would live at home when he went to the local university. This school was competitive and prestigious—there was no reason for Bart to go to an out-of-town college even if his parents could have afforded it.

But by the Thanksgiving break of Bart's freshman year, Hilary and Jack wished Bart had gone away to school — anywhere but in their town where they saw him on a daily basis. "In the old days, he used to tease us," Hilary recalls. "Sometimes the teasing had a bite to it, but it was never without humor or love. And we teased him back." No, Bart's teasing of them never even got close to being backtalk, Hilary insists. He was just "kidding around. There's a difference."

Ever since he started college, however, Bart's kidding had become backtalk. "This is what he said the first time he did it," Hilary recalled, eyes glassing over with tears. "We were sitting at the table, waiting for him to come home to dinner, when he burst in, arm around this girl, and said, 'What is this? You can't eat without me? You have to wait until I'm here? I'll be down in a couple of hours. Don't knock.'" With that, he and the girl, whom he never did introduce to his parents, went up to Bart's room, locked the door, and finally emerged at about 5:30 the next morning, when Hilary saw them sneaking silently out to the car. "I suspect he'd been drinking when he talked to us like that, but it hurt all the same," Hilary said.

Having been taken by surprise, Jack and Hilary had no idea how to react. After several more such incidents and a Thanksgiving holiday during which Bart backtalked steadily, blaming them for not being able to give him money for a ski trip all his college friends were enjoying over the holiday, they decided to enact a consequence.

"When Bart came home from classes the Monday after

Thanksgiving break, he found all his things on the lawn. I had packed them that morning. He was shocked. He said he needed time to find a place. We said, 'Go. Now.' There was no discussion. When he began to plead, saying he had nowhere to go, we turned and went back into the house. He followed us in and said he'd be nice to us from then on if he could stay. I replied that Jack had already turned his room into a home office."

Finally Bart had no recourse but to put his things in his car and take off. Did Bart turn to drugs, crime, or shady companions? Did he drop out of school? Did any of the other dire consequences predicted by Hilary's mother, Bart's mother, and several of their friends come to pass?

"Here's what happened," Hilary said. "Bart found three guys with an apartment who needed a roommate. Since there was only one bedroom, he had to sleep on the floor in the living room; the couch was already taken. Then he got a job in the student union busing tables to pay his share of the rent and utilities. The first semester, he got four F's and a B and was put on academic probation.

"By his junior year he was living in a dorm as a resident counselor, had raised his grade point average to a 3.0, and was working part-time as an intern for a government agency he hoped would hire him full-time upon his graduation. He then moved in with his steady girlfriend, whom he'd met while working in the student union. They're now engaged. None of this, Hilary added, is spectacular. But it's a lot better than what was happening to him in his freshman year. We believe our throwing him out forced him to take charge of his life in a way he might otherwise not have done for years."

Bart's backtalk was probably a sign of his need to individuate—become a person separate from his parents. Still, backtalk need not be the method used to accomplish this process.

If your child lives away from home, in an apartment or a dorm, be prepared for backtalk when she comes home for a visit. Children who go away from home to college often come back as different people on their first vacation break. Very often, these new people backtalk every chance they get, even in front of guests they bring home with them.

The Four-Step Program is clearly in order here. Choosing consequences, however, may prove challenging. It's not like designing consequences for a child who is still under your roof. A college student is an adult, with a will, a mind, and, in most cases, a car and a job of her own. Here are some ideas for consequences, some drastic, some mild, some in between.

DRASTIC CONSEQUENCES

- "That kind of talk is not acceptable in our house. Because of it, we do not want you staying here for the rest of your vacation. I expect you to be out of here in an hour." If the child is not out in an hour, pack up his things and put them in the yard.
- "That kind of talk is not acceptable to us.

Because of it, we are not enjoying having you this vacation. We'll be driving you back (or putting you on the plane) to your college tomorrow morning."

- "That kind of speech is not acceptable to us. We don't want to spend another vacation enduring the pain of it. Today we bought two tickets to Majorca, and we'll be leaving the first day of your next vacation. Aunt Hester and her parents will stay here while we're gone. Please make other arrangements for your vacation because you cannot come home."

MILD CONSEQUENCES

- "We feel bad because you said we do not read important books. To cheer ourselves up, we're going to the square dance in the park. Yes, we said you could take the car tonight, but we've decided to use it ourselves instead."
- "When you said all I care about is romance novels, I felt bad. To start feeling better, I'm spending all day tomorrow at the flower show. I know I said I'd cook for your high school reunion party, but I've decided it's more important for me to go to the flower show instead."

IN-BETWEEN CONSEQUENCES

- "We were hurt when you said in a condescending voice that our living room artwork was 'just decoration, not art,' and then you went on to criticize all the rest of the interior decoration in our house, which we have always enjoyed. So we don't want to spend any more time with you on this vacation. We've decided to spend the next two days on a guided tour of the art museum in Phoenix. Yes, we know we said you could have more company from school on those days, but since we won't be here, you will have to tell your friends to change their plans."

- "I don't like it when you tell me I'm a middle-aged consumerist housewife hooked into prime-time television, so I'm going to organize a theater party for every night during the rest of this holiday. Yes, I'll be taking the car. I'm sure you can make other arrangements for transportation and meals while you're here."

- "I didn't like hearing you say that my cooking is greasy, anachronistic, and perfunctory. So I'm not cooking anymore for you on this holiday. I know I said I'd make Thanksgiving dinner, but now I've decided to eat out."

As you know by now, you must follow through on these con-sequences and disengage from the struggle—quickly, because college students are the most persistent people in the world. They have been known to follow teachers down the hall, out of the building, and into their cars until they got the promise of a grade change. This is the same persistence that makes them camp out for days at a time to buy rock-concert tickets or go to Nepal for a ten-day trek with only $29.00 in their pocket, a pair of Reeboks, and six giant Hershey bars.

But cheer up. The Four-Step Program not only works with college children, it's the *only* thing that works.

12.

DEALING WITH BACKTALK FROM ADULT CHILDREN

If you have not yet dealt with your child's backtalk, remember that it's never too late to start. You must keep on dealing with backtalk if you expect to have a good relationship with your child as an adult. If you ignore it, you'll set the stage for a walking-on-eggs relationship with this child for the rest of your life.

Many adult children will try backtalk. There are at least three reasons why:

The Adult Wants to Go On Being Your Child. This child usually got his way during his formative years. Despite his bad treatment of you, he clearly enjoyed most-favored-person status in your life and has no intention of giving it up. His backtalk is his way of showing you he's still the boss. The following case history shows how this child's backtalk works—and what the best consequences for him can be.

Case History #18: Chad was the beloved only child of Jay and Carol. Nurtured and indulged, Chad grew up feeling empowered to be whatever he wanted—but also to talk rudely to his parents whenever he chose. After the parents' divorce, Chad became closer to his father, Jay, then ever. Upon his retirement, Jay began helping Chad in the latter's marketing business, making the fledgling firm a big success in just a few years. Then one day when Dad came to work, Chad told him to go home. Dad said he would just as soon stay in the office; it made him feel useful. In a shaming voice, Chad replied, "Dad, I don't want you coming here every day. Our company image is supposed to be young, dynamic—you kind of blow that when you're in the office."

Chad's receptionist, who was also his fiancée, was horrified. "How can you talk to your father like that?" she cried.

"Hey, Dad's used to it from me, his enfant terrible," Chad said fondly. "Besides, he likes me to tell him the hard truth. Don't you, Dad?"

Jay smiled. He left, all right. He went straight to his attorney's office, made arrangements to sever all his ties to Chad's company, and withdrew his financial investment. Chad, never having faced a consequence for his backtalk before, was stunned. He thought his father would reconsider. But Jay followed through on this consequence and disengaged from the struggle, not returning Chad's frantic telephone calls. Dad then went into business with a man his age and is doing fine. Chad is barely getting along and has seen his income cut by two-thirds.

The Adult Is Still Trying to Individuate. Adult children who backtalk for this reason are often extremely close to their parents. They call each other at least once a day and go on vacations together. Each one also brings the other along, uninvited, to social events because each is sure all the other people in their lives will also be thrilled to be with this parent or child.

But underneath all this happiness, the child is struggling to separate from her parents and become her own person; she needs to get away from this relationship. The struggle is terrible because it makes her feel guilty on the one hand and furious on the other. Case history #19 shows how this attempt to escape the closeness with a parent can take the form of backtalk.

Case History #19: Rilla and Nan had been at odds during Rilla's difficult teenage years, when Rilla lived with her remarried father. However, Rilla did not get along with the stepmother, a woman not much older than she, and moved back in with her mother.

For various reasons, probably having to do with Nan's loneliness and Rilla's feeling of having been replaced by the stepmother in her father's heart, Rilla and her mother became like sisters. They began wearing the same outfits, doing their hair the same way, spending all their free time together. When friends invited Nan to lunch or a movie, she showed up with her daughter in tow. If Nan found that her friends were not overly glad to see Rilla, Nan became angry and stopped seeing them. She and Rilla became such a package deal that Nan had no life of her own during the years Rilla was living with her. But, as Nan told the few old friends who still kept in touch, she thought it was for the best. Rilla seemed to be getting the parenting and nurturing she had missed during her childhood, and she was approaching life with a new self-confidence. Sure enough, Rilla got a good job with a hospital not long after she graduated from the local community college and was immediately transferred to the West Coast.

About six months later, looking forward to a lovely reunion with this daughter whose company she now missed very much, Nan went to visit Rilla. Rilla met her at the airport with a young man, also an employee of the hospital.

"Now, don't get ideas about him and me," Rilla ordered her mother while the man was waiting to pick up Nan's luggage.

"I wasn't about to have any ideas," Nan said, laughing, thinking Rilla was joking.

"I know how you are," Rilla snapped angrily. "You always have to stick your nose into everything I do, know about everyone I see."

"Rilla dear . . . " Nan began, stricken with hurt and shame.

"Well, you're not going to be that way here," Rilla went on curtly. "Now, hurry up, don't dawdle. And I hope you brought a lighter coat than that fake fur. It's much too hot here for that heavy old thing."

"Maybe you could take me shopping here," Nan suggested hopefully.

"Mother, if you don't know what to shop for by now, forget it. I'm not going to hold your hand through your whole life!"

This kind of backtalk continued, and increased, as the visit wore on. Not knowing what else to do, Nan endured it on this visit. But on the next visit, a year later, she knew what to do. On Rilla's first attack at the airport, Nan said, "That kind of talk is not acceptable to me, dear. So, I won't be staying with you or seeing you on this trip. Next time I come out, I hope we can spend time together."

With that, she kissed her stunned daughter good-bye and took a taxi to the Disneyland Hotel. Having been fairly sure that this would happen, she had made a reservation at that hotel several months before. She did not tell Rilla where she would be staying, and once she processed her sadness about not being able to be with her daughter, she had a terrific visit to Disneyland.

Many of Nan's friends think she took too big a risk. But she knows that her relationship with Rilla was not respectful. The backtalk was unbearable and destructive and had to be changed no matter what.

Rilla's backtalk was due, Nan sees now, to the need to have a life away from her mother. Rilla was probably frightened that her mother would want to be too much a part of this fledgling new life that she was beginning to enjoy. She knew very well that Nan was now alone, was not having a social life, and had still not replaced her daughter's company. But while Rilla may have been within her rights to keep her mother at a distance, she was not right to do it with abusive backtalk.

The Adult Grew Up in a Household in Which at Least One Parent Was an Alcoholic or in Some Other Way Out of Control. Backtalk is a means of controlling others. If a child can make another person feel bad whenever he wants, he can control what that person thinks, feels, and does. The next case history shows backtalk by an adult that may have been caused by a parent's alcoholism.

Case History #20: Chet was an active alcoholic from the time his two children were in grade school until they finished high school. Then he joined Alcoholics Anonymous, stopped drinking completely, and has been sober ever since. The days when he was drinking, throwing furniture around, disappearing for periods of time, and threatening the family with violence when he did come home, were never discussed and were supposedly forgotten. His wife, Arlene, told everyone that the kids had put the old days out of their minds and gone on to be more successful and well adjusted than any other children she knew. Chet Junior was admitted to an Ivy League college and became an internist; his brother, Paul, who went through the Eastman School of Music, became a teacher in an affluent Long Island public high school. Both married women in their fields, a nurse practitioner and a violinist, respectively, and went on to own beautiful homes, take trips, and have successful lives. Arlene and Chet's only regret was that Chet Junior was soon given a job as chief surgeon in a hospital several hundred miles away—but they were sure they would visit often. Chet's wife called soon after they moved to announce that she was expecting. Arlene decided she would postpone visiting until the baby's birth.

"I thought everything was perfect," Arlene said. "It was as if I had everything the way I wanted it—until Chet Junior called to tell me I couldn't come visit when the baby was born."

His mother couldn't be present during what was one of the biggest events of her life? "He said, I just didn't fit in," Arlene recalled. "I didn't look right, I didn't act right, and I would make his wife nervous." Arlene knew his wife was from a very wealthy family, but she had not realized this woman was so judgmental.

"Yes," Arlene added when asked, her eyes filling with tears, "he used those very words. My own son! The pain was beyond belief." But she said she should have been prepared a few years back when he gave her a list of things she had to do before she attended his wedding, such as lose weight, get her hair colored and styled a certain way, and buy a wedding outfit in a color to coordinate with the rest of the bridal party.

A therapist told Arlene later that the wedding instructions should indeed have been a warning. "The therapist said asking me to wear a certain color of outfit was legitimate, but the other instructions were very controlling."

When Arlene got angry at Chet Junior for his serious backtalk, he blew up at her. "He just started screaming awful things at me. He went beyond backtalk. It was exactly the sort of thing his father used to do to me when he was drunk."

So far, this case history has not had a happy ending. Arlene has asked and been granted permission to see the baby a month before the child's first birthday. She was not invited to the first birthday party, nor did she ask to attend it. Arlene plans to care for herself (a common phrase from the Alcoholics Anonymous canon) by going to see the baby, which she desperately wants to do, but by leaving if Chet Junior starts backtalking her. "It kind of reminds me of how my life was with his father during the drinking days. I don't know what's going to be said or not said. My son acts like his father did, even though he's not an alcoholic."

Arlene hopes her son will not start backtalking. She wants to be with the baby as long as she can.

Why do the children of alcoholics have such a need to control? Partly because control is all they know. The alcoholic controlled their lives for so long with his decisions to drink, often on the most inappropriate occasions, such as birthdays, graduations, and other important events when sobriety was most counted upon. The alcoholic also controlled how family members felt, by using verbal and physical abuse. The child learned control subconsciously. Even if an alcoholic parent quits drinking or leaves the family, the child's need to control almost always continues, until he recognizes it and gets some kind of help.

Other reasons why children of alcoholics exhibit controlling behavior are beyond the scope of this book. But it is easy to see how hurtful backtalk can come tumbling out of the mouths of the most devoted children—if they grew up with an alcoholic parent.

The messages of this chapter have been that adult children will engage in backtalk; that their backtalk is especially hurtful because they are adults whose friendship parents so much want after all the years of nurturing; and that enacting consequences usually involves removing oneself—temporarily, one hopes—from the children's presence. No other consequences, such as not driving them to a friend's house, work at this stage of the children's life.

This removal of oneself often helps the parent, too. It enables her to see that she must develop a life away from her adult children if she does not already have one. Does the child respond to this consequence and stop talking back? Unless the parent has done something totally unforgivable to the child in his earlier life, the answer is almost always yes.

13.

RESOURCES

Unless you live in the most underpopulated area imaginable, finding a parenting group is relatively easy. Check the business pages in your local phone book under "Parent" or "Social and Human Services" to see what you find. You may discover your city not only has a publication just for parents (our town has two!) but a special center that offers parenting groups and classes. You can also call local school administrations, toy and children's clothing shops, and churches.

You will benefit greatly from joining a parenting group that shares the beliefs taught in this book. To find out if it does, ask the group leader two questions:

1. Is the group based on the principles of Alfred Adler and Rudolf Dreikurs?
2. Is it a STEP (Systematic Training for Effective Parenting) group?

If the group leader answers no to these questions but assures you her group "will be just as beneficial," join at your own risk. Perhaps it will be just as beneficial—if it shares your views on backtalk. If it does not, this group could soon weaken the backbone you've developed for dealing with backtalk. In the wrong group, you could begin to experience the following:

Doubt. Should you really be trying to change your child's natural verbal expression? He's just trying to communicate.

Fear. Enacting consequences could cause your child to act out in ways that are very self-destructive.

Confusion. "Wait a minute," you keep wanting to say to the group members. "When I say I am responding to my child's misbehavior, you say I'm insensitive to the child. When I let my child behave however he wants, you say I'm not giving enough guidance. I'm confused!" But you will not say these things because you want the approval of the group members.

Insecurity. The group members with the more dominant personalities will say that their children never talk back. If yours do, they must be deficient in some way. You feel insecure about your ability to even produce satisfactory children, let alone raise them.

Self-pity. Most time in this group is taken up with lamentations about things children have done to hurt parents. You find yourself joining right in, complaining louder and more articulately than anyone. After a few sessions, however, you begin to buy into your complaints and feel *really* put upon in a way you never did before.

All these feelings are produced for one main reason: the group lacks a strong philosophical orientation and so falls prey to the beliefs of its most controlling members. Since these members are seldom professionals, their beliefs can change direction like the wind, depending on whom they talk to or what they read or see on television. And, having changed, they often deny the previous belief. "Of course I was always progressive with my children," one member will insist, completely forgetting—or being unwilling to remember— that she was a staunch disciplinarian just two days before.

Groups that are committed to a philosophy can still be flexible. But they use that philosophy as a framework through which they can examine problems of the members. Adlerian philosophy, for instance, includes the idea that respectful behavior is very important in families. Thus, backtalk is examined through the framework of respect and seen to be not respectful. If examined through educator A. S. Neill's framework of self-expression, backtalk would appear to be creative, exciting, dynamic, and healthy. While we cannot agree with this framework, we're sure you can find sources and authorities who will. But you should decide if this approach is what you really want.

DETERMINING A GROUP'S PHILOSOPHY

If a group espouses no recognizable philosophy or theoretical framework, it will reveal its current beliefs in answers to certain questions. Don't hesitate to ask the group leader or members what you want to know. For instance:

- Ask them outright how they feel about backtalk. If they look at one another or hesitate as though unfamiliar with the topic, be wary. If the leader says something like "Well, it depends on the child and the circumstances," be wary.
- Ask them if they condone spanking. If you get the "It depends on the circumstances" kind of answer, you can be assured this is not a group based on the philosophy of Adler and Dreikurs.
- Ask which books on child rearing they recommend. If they say none in particular, you'll know there is no one philosophical focus to this group. If many of the following titles are among those they do recommend, you can be fairly sure this group's ideas will be compatible with yours.

Cline, Foster W., and Jim Fay. *Parenting with Love and Logic: Teaching Children Responsibility*. Navpress, 1990.

Dinkmeyer, Don C., and Gary D. McKay. *Parenting Teenagers: Systematic Training for Effective Parenting*. American Guidance Service, 1989. Revised edition, paperback: New York: Random House, 1990.

Dinkmeyer, Don C., and Gary D. McKay. *The Parent's Handbook: Systematic Training for Effective Parenting*. American Guidance Service, 1989. Paperback: New York: Random House, 1997.

Dinkmeyer, Don C., and Gary D. McKay. *Raising a*

Responsible Child: How to Prepare Your Child for Today's Complex World. New York: Simon & Schuster, 1973. Revised and updated edition, paperback: New York: Fireside (Simon & Schuster), 1996.

Dinkmeyer, Don C.; Gary D. McKay; and James S. Dinkmeyer. *New Beginnings: Skills for Single Parents and Stepfamily Parents*. Champaign, Ill.: Research Press, 1987.

Dinkmeyer, Don C., ed.; Gary D. McKay; and James S. Dinkmeyer. *Parenting Young Children: Systematic Training for Effective Parenting (STEP) of Children Under Six*. American Guidance Service, 1989. Paperback: Random House, 1997.

Dreikurs, Rudolf. *The Challenge of Parenthood*. Reprint edition, paperback: New York: Plume, 1992.

Dreikurs, Rudolf; Pearl Cassel, and David Kehoe. *Discipline Without Tears*. Reprint edition, paperback: New York: Plume, 1992.

Dreikurs, Rudolf, and Loren Grey. *A New Approach to Discipline: Logical Consequences*. New York: Penguin, 1993.

Dreikurs, Rudolf, and Loren Grey. *A Parent's Guide to Child Discipline*. New York: Hawthorn, 1970.

Dreikurs, Rudolf, and Vickie Soltz. *Children: The Challenge*. New York: Dutton, 1964. Reissue edition, paperback: New York: Plume, 1991.

Nelsen, Jane; Cheryl Erwin; and Carol Delzer. *Positive Discipline for Single Parents: A Practical Guide to Raising Children Who Are Responsible, Respectful, and Resourceful*. Rocklin, Calif.: Prima, 1993.

Nelsen, Jane; Cheryl Erwin, and Roslyn Duffy. *Positive Discipline for Preschoolers*. Rocklin, Calif.: Prima, 1994.

Nelsen, Jane, ed.; Lynn Lott, and H. Stephen Glenn. *Positive Discipline A–Z: 1001 Solutions to Everyday Parenting Problems*. Rocklin, Calif.: Prima, 1993.

If the group does not seem to share your philosophy and backtalk beliefs but consists of members you like, you might want to join and stick to your own agenda. Share your progress with your backtalk program; others might be interested in participating. Avoid, however, trying to convert anyone; you would not want that process tried on you.

STARTING YOUR OWN PARENTING GROUP

If there are no parenting groups in your area, try forming one of your own. Decide on a meeting place (preferably a room in a church or other public place), a meeting day, and a time. Do not provide your personal telephone number; it's never a good idea to make your personal phone number public. If possible, use the number of an inexpensive answering service or a cooperative business.

Choose a book from the list in this chapter for members to use as a basic text. The group could focus on just one topic, such as backtalk, or on whatever topic any member at any meeting finds most pressing. The philosophy of the text, however, should be used as a guide for discussion. The problem should be examined through the framework of the text's philosophy.

Post notices of the meeting on church bulletin boards and in hospital cafeterias, teachers' lounges, and public and university libraries. Send notices to newspapers and television and radio stations that broadcast public service announcements.

Have simple refreshments available at your first meeting. If no one attends, schedule one more meeting before you give up.

Here is an example of a notice for a new group:

> Interested in talking about child-raising?
> A parent's discussion group is forming now.
> First meeting will be held
> from 10:00 to 11:30 a.m.
> on Thursday, January 3, in Meeting Room A-2 of
> The Midvale Public Library.
> Text to be used: *Discipline Without Tears* by
> Dreikurs and Cassel (New York: Penguin, 1991),
> available at the library.
> Child care will not be provided.
> Light refreshments will be served.
> Please come. We'd love to meet you.

You will be tempted to tell parents they can bring children to the meeting, but it is not a good idea. Parents can't focus with children running around.

If you prefer, specify an age group to be discussed, such as preschoolers or middle schoolers or teens.

At the first meeting, introduce yourself, tell why you wanted to form a group, why you have chosen the particular text, what parenting issue is most important to you right now, and why. Then ask the attendees to volunteer their first names, the ages of their children, the parenting issues they want to discuss, and any other information they want to share.

At this point you can ask if anyone has a particularly pressing problem. Surely someone will volunteer one, but if not, you should be prepared to do so. By now you'll probably have a fairly lively conversation flowing. Don't overlook quieter group members. They may simply need some friendly encouragement. Try to establish a regular meeting time for your group, and make sure everyone gets a chance to participate.

If the entire group is willing to deal with backtalk, terrific. You can use *this* book as a text!

14.

QUESTIONS FROM
PARENTS ABOUT
BACKTALK

When people found out we were writing *Backtalk*, we were very often asked specific questions about children's backtalk.

We decided to include some of these questions here, in a last chapter, along with our answers.

Why does my son, age seven, use the worst kind of backtalk when I first pick him up from the day care center after working all day? What can I do about it? We've been very satisfied with the center and can't see any reason for this behavior.

Your son is probably picking up backtalk from other children whose parents don't discourage it. You deal with this backtalk the same way you'd deal with any backtalk. Tell him his behavior is not acceptable, that in this case it's exhausting energy you certainly do not have, and as a result, you are not doing something he expects you to do. Before you pick him up after work again, choose a consequence. When he begins the backtalk, enact the consequence, and disengage from his struggle. If you're in the habit of stopping for a treat on the way home, not stopping would be an excellent consequence. So would not doing something you usually do for him when you get home every day. You'll think of others. Reading this book, especially chapters 7 and 8, should give you more ideas.

Our son, age ten, bombards us with really awful backtalk whenever we take his video game away. He's so bad I just let him go on playing way past the time I've allowed for playing. What should I do?

Remind him he agreed to certain hours of video game play. Tell him that because his behavior is unacceptable, and as a result of playing video games, he can't play them at all the next day. Enact that consequence the next day, and disengage from the struggle that is sure to follow. The day after, he can play the video games as usual. If he backtalks again when the time comes to stop playing, do not allow him to play the next day.

My husband is very permissive with the kids. Our son and daughter, age nine and twelve, are becoming backtalkers par excellence. My husband thinks they're cute, and I can't impose any discipline because the kids know he'll give in and say yes to whatever they want. Is there anything I can do?

Children eventually discover that all adults do not think or behave the same way. In fact, it's good for them to see adults be happy together even though they do not agree. Set aside a time to discuss this problem with your mate, possibly over dinner in a restaurant. Acknowledge your differences in attitude. Tell him the children need consistency. Negotiate an agreement on backtalk. If he doesn't honor that agreement, institute your own backtalk-prevention program. Tell your husband you'll help him deal with backtalk when he decides he does not like it either. Meanwhile, proceed with the Four-Step Program taught in this book. Soon your husband may be so impressed with the respectful treatment your children give you that he may try it. How another adult responds to backtalk need not be your concern. If none of your efforts are effective and your husband won't honor your agreement, you might want to seek counseling. You could have a separate marital issue in addition to the backtalk problem.

My daughter, age fourteen, has this silent smirking method of getting her way, and it drives me crazy. Her technique consists of smiles and laughter that make the rest of us feel so out of it, so ridiculous and silly, that we give in right away and hope her opinion of us will change. But every time I call her on her behavior, she says she wasn't laughing, or wasn't laughing at me, and there's no way I can prove she was. Help!

You don't have to prove anything. You treat smirking and laughter for the nonverbal backtalk they actually are. Tell her that her behavior is upsetting to you, enact your chosen consequence, and ignore her indignant protests that you're paranoid, crazy, overreacting, and abusive. She'll soon learn that smirking does not work with you!

I have been trying out your program with success. My child, age eleven, thinks twice about talking back to me now. Her mouth will open and she'll start to say "Whatever," which has always been her favorite retort, and she'll stop herself from saying it because she knows what the consequence will be, my refusal to drive her to the place where she needs to be taken that day—and she needs to be taken to at least one place, sometimes several, every day!

My problem is that I want to make her admit the consequence worked, and I want to remind her of it without having to enact it. I don't like this tendency in myself at all. Is this natural?

Yes. It's a trait, albeit one of the least attractive traits, of human nature to want to rub things in. It's a way of asserting power over another human being. But it won't work with your backtalk program because it'll make the child want to get back at you. Instead of getting her to look at her own behavior to see how she can avoid unwanted consequences by rubbing it in you could make your daughter regard you as an enemy who must be defeated. She'll have to fight back against you. She could begin misbehaving in other ways just to let you know you're not as powerful as you think.

Here is the sort of dialogue that can take place if you rub in your success with your backtalk program:

Parent: Watch what you say, young lady. Remember what happened the last time you said "Whatever" to me? And the time before that? I'll do the same thing again if you say something I don't like.

Daughter: (Silence)

Parent: Do you hear me?

Daughter: Whatever.

Parent: What did you say?

Daughter: You heard me. And I don't care if you never drive me anywhere again. I'll get my own rides from now on!

It is not only better to enact the consequence and say nothing, it is necessary to your success at curbing backtalk. Rubbing-in the consequence with words makes the consequence a punishment.

This program is not about exacting punishment or getting revenge. It's about enacting consequences of children's behavior that are logical. This cannot be repeated enough: The child who knows that Behavior A will bring about Consequence B will begin figuring out how she can control her own behavior. This self-control on her part will undoubtedly have the consequence for parents and child of a much happier, more productive life.

I am dating a widower who has four college-age children. They all came home for their father's birthday and were delighted when he offered to treat them to a day at Disneyland. But when we got there, the youngest daughter, Ariel, got cranky. When her father begged her not to go into one of her moods, she just shrugged. When he suggested we all start out with breakfast, she said "Whatever" in this mean tone. Then she said something in the same tone to one of her sisters, but we couldn't hear what it was. All the kids laughed in this derisive way. "Ariel, what did you say?" her dad asked, mad.

"Nothing," she replied in a tone of injured innocence. "Why are you giving me a hard time?" Her dad ignored that reply and tried to act as if everything were fine. But everything was not fine. Ariel's comments seemed to inspire the other kids to get sarcastic, and they ruined the day. Her father and I had such a hard time holding our tempers and trying to be cheerful. What should her father have done?

The father should have told the children that that kind of talk was not enjoyable to him, so he and you were going to go off on your own. Then that's exactly what the two of you should have done. The four grown children could have taken care of themselves and found their own way home.

A friend of mine whom I had not seen for fifteen years was wheeling her three-year-old granddaughter in the supermarket. The two of us were delighted to see each other. This woman reported that her three children were now grown, married, and very successful. I was glad to hear that because they were always such polite and respectful children.

Then, while we were talking, the granddaughter began carrying on. "Go, Grandma!" she ordered in a very imperious tone. "I want fute loops!"

The woman stopped talking with me and said sternly to the child, "I'm talking!" Then she returned to the conversation with me, ignoring the pleading child. Was this a good thing to do?

Yes. She did not give in to the child's demands, and she assumed the child could handle the consequence she enacted, which was removing her attention (if not herself physically, which you cannot do with a child that age in a public place) from the child. This assumption shows respect for the child's capabilities at the same time it allows the enactment of the consequence. No wonder this woman's own children were so respectful to others!

INDEX